EDITING HL

Challenges to Faith posed by the Biological Sciences

David Atkinson

British Library Cataloguing in Publication Data:
a catalogue record for this publication
is available from the British Library

ISBN   978-1-912052-57-8

© David Atkinson 2020

The right of David Atkinson to be identified
as the author of this work has been asserted by him
in accordance with the Copyright, Designs and Patents Act 1988

Most Scripture quotations are taken from the Revised English Bible
© Cambridge University Press and Oxford University Press 1989

Typeset in 11.5pt Minion Pro at Haddington, Scotland

Printing and cover design by
West Port Print and Design, St Andrews

The illustration on the back cover is a photograph taken while walking on the Frank Bruce Sculpture Trail, Feshie Bridge, Invernessshire. Entitled *The Millennium*, it is of one of his wonderful carved sculptures; its symbolism set against the beautiful natural setting would seem to encompass the world in our hands, and the responsibility this brings.

Acknowledgements

The coming into being of this volume owes much to friends and colleagues too numerous to mention by name but I am grateful to all of the many people with whom I have discussed ideas for this venture and who have encouraged me to continue. Over the years I have been a member of too many committees but I have learned from them all and they have severally informed what is here.

Some people have had a major role. My partner Margaret has proof read the manuscript and has allowed me to use some of her poems and reflections. For conversations over many years I would like to thank Donald and Ann Bruce with whom I have worked over a period of almost three decades. I thank Martin Auld and Richard Murray for discussions around environmental issues, Dr Richard Johnson for discussion on just so many issues and for a detailed reading of the manuscript, and Dr Hilary Constable for being brave enough to provide formative comments on an earlier draft.

It would certainly never have come about without the colleagues who made up the Scottish Episcopal Church's 'Church in Society Working Group' on Genome Editing, its convenor Dr Donald Bruce and its regular members Dr Ann Bruce, Prof. Kenneth Boyd, Dr Lesley Penny, Dr Murdo MacDonald, Prof. Jim Mckillop (who also commented on a draft), Prof. Bruce Whitelaw.

It also owes much to the 'Ireland and UK Bioethics Group' – to its chair Brendan McCarthy, to Bishop James Newcombe, and to Rory Corbett. The support of the Revd Prof. Keith Suckling (who commented on a draft), and is a member of the SEC 'Church in Society Committee', is also gratefully acknowledged. I thank also the Handsel Press and its editor Jock Stein.

The initial thoughts for the talks which led to this volume arose from conversations with the Provost of St Andrew's Cathedral Aberdeen, the Very Revd Dr Isaac Poobalan, Dr Amu Poobalan and Prof. Ferdinand von Prondzynski on the role of a cathedral in today's Scotland, and with colleagues in the Donside Ministry Team – the Revd Canon John Walker, Mr Nigel Fielden, Mrs Avril Hern.

Glossary

(*means that definitions are expanded in Chapter 12)

ACE2 Angiotensin Converting Enzyme 2

ASF African Swine Fever

AI Artificial Intelligence

AIDS Acquired Immune Deficiency Syndrome, the disease caused by the HIV virus

BAME Black Asian Minority Ethnic

Base The individual components of DNA also known as nucleotides or letters. Their arrangement determines the genetic code

BCE Before the Common Era (a term which has replaced BC, Before Christ)

Belief A firmly held conviction sometimes in the absence of scientific evidence

Cas9 A protein utilised in Genome Editing to cut DNA and critical to the ability of bacteria to protect against viral infection

CE Common Era a term which has replaced AD, Anno Domini

Cloning* Production of individuals with a genome identical to earlier individuals

Codon Three bases in a particular order which specify an amino acid

Cohort Studies* A programme begun in 1946 to follow individuals born in the same week over the course of their lives

Covid19* The disease caused by the Corona virus SARS-CoV-2

CRISPR* Clustered Regularly Interspaced Short Palindromic Repeats: the main Genome Editing tool

DNA* Deoxyribonucleic acid

DNR Do Not Resuscitate

DPP Director of Public Prosecutions

Epigenetics* How the expression of genes is modified and regulated in a way which allows cells with the same genes to be functionally divergent

Eucaryote Higher more complex organisms such as plants and animals where the DNA is separated from cytoplasm by a membrane

Evolution* *Theory* proposed by Charles Darwin to account for the development of all living things through selection of the fittest and which explains the fossil record

Extinction Rebellion A Climate Change action group which came into existence in 2018 inspired by the views of Greta Thunberg

Fact An empirical repeatable observation

Gene A sequence of DNA which codes for a protein

Genesis The first book in the Old Testament

Genome The genetic material of an organism, the sum total of DNA

Genome Editing* A generic term for approaches, of which CRISPR is the most common, to alter the genome of an organism

GM* Genetically Modified, a synonym of Genetically Engineered. An approach to adding additional genes, frequently from other organisms, to the genome of a target organism, most commonly a crop plant

HeLa* Cell culture derived from Henrietta Lack's cervical tumour

HFEA Human Fertilisation and Embryology Authority

HIV/AIDS Human Immunodeficiency Virus

Human Genome Project* A complete read out of the human genome, an average genome with which variations can be compared

Hypothesis Testable speculations which can explain facts, a testable idea

Inherent Properties A feature e.g. 'Organic food' related to how it was produced but undetectable by physical or chemical analysis

IVF* In Vitro Fertilisation, the process which led to the first test tube baby (and in a modified version to Dolly the sheep)

Leviticus The third book in the Old Testament

Lockdown A Government Prescribed Social Distancing response to Covid19 requiring everyone to stay at home

LGBT Lesbian Gay Bisexual Transgender

Metaphor A descriptive term for something not being used in a physical or scientific sense

OED Oxford English Dictionary

Organ Transplantation* The transfer of organs from one individual to another initially done using kidneys and hearts

PCR Polymerase Chain Reaction, a molecular tool used in characterising genotype

PGD Pre-implantation Genetic Diagnosis

PPE Personal Protective Equipment

Prokaryote A simple organism, such as a bacterium, where its DNA or RNA is not surrounded by a nuclear membrane

Ribosomes* A structure critical to life and found in every cell, and the machine by which RNA is able to manufacture proteins

Polio Vaccination* The developments needed to reduce the global extent of infantile paralysis caused by the Polio virus

RNA* Ribonucleic acid which occurs as messenger, (mRNA) ribosomal (rRNA) and transfer (tRNA)

SARS-CoV-2 The virus causing Covid19

SEC Scottish Episcopal Church, a part of the Post-Reformation 'Church of Scotland', the Anglican Communion in Scotland

Stem Cells* Cells which are able to produce new cells like themselves or less commonly any type of new cell

Theory A coherent conceptual model that explains whole sets of facts and that withstands the falsifying of testable predictions

Vaccination See Polio vaccination

Virus* An 'organism' made of RNA with a protein coat and which is responsible for human diseases such as Covid 19, Flu and Polio

Contents

Preface

We are living in an age of hitherto unimagined technological innovation and scientific advances but also of increasing challenges to the place of Scripture, Faith and 'how God fits into all of this'. However, the combined tsunami-like impact of new Science, Covid19 and Climate Change affects the meaning of 'being human' in ways the world is finding it hard to contemplate. Margaret Harris from WHO said on BBC's Today Programme on 23rd June 2020, '*We are entering an era of living differently which means for us all we will have to adopt and adapt to "the new normal" to survive.*' This provides a window onto the inherent question at the heart of this Book, 'What Does it Mean to be Human?'

This is a question that may be answered in many ways. It raises issues traditionally considered as matters of life and death such as when does human life begin and when does death happen? Developments in the biological and medical sciences have made these concerns more complex. We are all a product of our genetic makeup and a range of environmental factors. We have long known that we can change the environment and by doing so increase the length and quality of life. We are becoming increasingly aware of the ways in which environment governs the expression of our genetics. Prior to the development of Genome Editing our genetics were not something we could change. Much of modern medicine was there to counter adverse consequences of our genetics but the genome we had was the genome we were stuck with.

Then came the opening window of CRISPR and its potential for improved amelioration of the genetic problems of the present. However, it also posed the thought that it might be possible to change the nature of people in the future. The birth of two particular girls in China in late 2018 made this prospect a reality. Discoveries about the impact of epigenetics, our functional genetics, added to this. Many questions raised by Science Fiction had become real possibilities, now and in the foreseeable future. All of these advances came at a time when we were concerned about the impact of Climate Change and had accepted that life could not go on as it had. We needed to change. Covid19 amplified this need many times over. The advent of Covid19 and the impact of this virus and perhaps of other viruses in the future, has caused us to reflect on our vision for our species even more urgently. Yes, there are things that we might wish to do biologically but the response to Covid19 has caused us to think beyond physical attributes.

For many, and especially people of faith, it has re-opened questions about purpose, where is God at such times and to seek guidance in the wisdom of Scripture. Scripture describes a journey of faith. It was not linier. It was messy but the strength of the relationship between humanity and God deepened. An increasing richness of experience brought increasing wisdom. Almost two thousand years have passed since the events detailed in the Bible. Humanity's journey has continued. New experiences have added to the deepening of the relationship with God and have brought new insights. This continues to be true. Modern biology and other current issues have the potential to change life as it is being lived but they also have the potential to provide a further deepening of our relationship with God and to provide a means of a new generation establishing such a relationship and in perhaps a different way. In this book questions are asked about wider values and why 'What it Means to be Human' has once again become a question that we need to re-address in both scientific and scriptural terms.

Dedication

This volume is dedicated to my partner Margaret
without whose continuing support and challenge
it would never have been as it is or even completed.

Chapter 1

First Thoughts

Imagine a world where humankind had the powers of Marvel Super Heroes, were resistant to all virus diseases and were able to direct the evolution of every living thing. Such a world has long been the vision of the writers of Science Fiction. Could that be a prospect in the foreseeable future? Genome Editing technologies such as CRISPR seem to hold that out as a reality. Will Genome Editing really rewrite our futures in the ways that have been suggested?[1] If they could, would we have the wisdom to make the right choices? Do our genes represent all that is important in 'what it means to be human'? Where does Faith sit in all of this? Has Covid19 made all of this unimportant? These are among the issues explored in this book.

So, what am I aiming to do in this book? Well, at its most basic level I aim to explore how the new and sometimes revolutionary bioscience techniques, such as CRISPR, which allow changes to be made to our genetic codes, sit alongside both earlier science and the age-old issues around 'what it means to be human'. Without doubt, for mankind, these new techniques are potentially beneficial and challenging, and in their most extreme form could be classed as playing at being God. Such developments may prove hard to accept for people of faith and yet, were such techniques to be seen to have personal benefit, then the choice of acceptance can become more complex – after all 'we are all only human!'

Thoughts about the meaning of humanity and the purpose of life have perhaps been more common and more deeply felt during the early months of 2020 than at any time since the end of the two major World Wars of the Twentieth Century. Warning signs that there were serious challenges ahead appeared in late 2019 with the emergence of a new virus in Wuhan in China which, by the beginning of 2020, seemed to have spread to a number of other countries in Asia and then to Italy and other parts of Europe including the UK. Covid19 has changed life and resulted in a major

---

1 Carey N (2020), *Hacking the Code of Life,* Icon Books, London.

reassessment of what is important and which of the things that we value rank as the most important. It is clear that in a real sense life post Covid19 will be very different to life before the arrival of the virus.

More than perhaps anything else, Covid19 has damaged our confidence in our ability to take decisions both at a personal level and as a society. Writing this as we come out of Lockdown it's clear that a majority in society in the UK remain nervous about going out into indoor public spaces such as restaurants, while Government decisions on what we can and cannot do change dramatically from day to day. This impacts on all aspects of life but gives added dimensions in areas such as the potential impact and role of new information like those being generated in the biological and the related medical sciences. Developments in these areas posed new and difficult ethical and scientific challenges before the advent of Covid19 but the advent of this virus has both raised new questions and has changed the importance of some questions which were already being discussed.

Prior to the advent of Covid19 the most important global questions being asked within society as a whole were probably those linked to Climate Change. There was a growing awareness that our lifestyles and the patterns of resource use by humanity were for the first time ever changing the conditions for *all* life on our planet. In parallel with the clear call to modify the ways in which we live and our demands on the planet there have been other challenges. Developments in our understanding of our genetic code, which greatly impacts on who we are, have moved to a point where editing our own genetic make-up using the newly developed CRISPR technology has become a real possibility. This raises the Spectre or the Opportunity of being able to direct the evolution of humanity and other species. CRISPR has the potential to change the debate about health. In doing so it has re-asked long-standing questions about personal identity and how we regard those with differences which might be classed as disabilities. It also questioned our relationships to other living creatures and our responsibilities for directing their evolution.

Scripture tells us of a series of journeys in faith, the development of the early church within the challenges of the Roman world, the re-establishment of Israel after the return from Babylon and the journey from Egypt to the promised land. John Bunyan's *Pilgrims Progress* also describes a journey in which the pilgrim is challenged to deal with situations and decisions as part of that life's journey. In the same sense dealing with the issues of the modern world is also a pilgrimage. Science throws up new possibilities some of which might change the world as we have known it. Like Bunyan's pilgrim we need to respond. Doing so will be influenced by how we regard and understand Science and for those with a Faith how this might be guided by Scripture and our faith journey.

The word pilgrimage for many will lead to an image of a journey such as that taken by Chaucer's Pilgrims going from London to Canterbury. However, in that pilgrimage and most others, participants both learn about themselves and increase their understanding of their stance in respect to the issues encountered on the journey. In his book *Earth Pilgrim*[2] the Buddhist philosopher Satish Kumar explores the role of pilgrimage in personal development and in promoting a greater connection with the world in which we live. He suggested that ultimately everything is linked, connected, related with nothing being completely independent. Bees are important to themselves and to us. Without bees there would be no life. We all depend on other organisms. In that sense there is no 'I' as an unrelated entity. We are all on a pilgrimage, through life and through a journey, an exploration, with the rest of life. However, each journey has its own purpose. That purpose does not need to have a clear destination although initial purpose can be needed to provide the impetus to begin and to open the eyes to what might be seen when journeying. At times we all need practical motivation.

Coming from this we can ask do we see ourselves, humanity, as an integral part of the world or do we see ourselves as sitting outside the world but making decisions about the planet and other living things?

Science, Scripture and Covid19

This book discusses recent developments in Science but it is not just about Science. The book discusses the role of Scripture in guiding life in the current world, but it does not aim to be a contemporary commentary on Scripture. Throughout the book there are many references to Covid19 but it is not an attempt to look at the Covid pandemic through the lens of Scripture. This has recently been done by the former Bishop of Durham.[3]

---

2 Kumar S (2009) *Earth Pilgrim*, Green Books, Totness, Devon.

3 Wright NT (2020) *God and the Pandemic: A Christian reflection on the coronavirus and the aftermath*, SPCK, London.

He concluded that it was necessary for the church to rediscover the theme of Lament. He suggested that Psalms 72 and 73 taken together contrast the importance of the poor and needy within the Divine agenda with the apparent success of the rich and powerful. They seem to suggest how things are but with a glimpse of how they could be. There seemed to be a need for someone to appear with a vision for the future and a plan for how it might be achieved. We needed another Joseph, an issue discussed again in chapter 10.

In this book my aim is to identify issues which have their roots in the biological sciences, have the potential to fundamentally change the world as we have known it and where there is need, to ask whether Scripture and the practise of faith provide us with guidance as to how we might deal with the issue. In this context Covid19 becomes important because it asks hard questions about our ability to function as a species under threat, our ability to learn from the past and the present and our willingness to make use of such learning. It has also asked questions about how we understand Science and its role in providing solutions in such circumstances.

There have always been inequalities in society. Some inequalities we have attempted to minimise through social measures. Covid19 has shown up the consequences of inequalities we have failed to neutralise and has thus asked questions of our societal values. In a very stark way, it has questioned our collective wisdom. Climate Change had already begun to undermine our sense of having sufficient understanding, of being sufficiently in control. Genome Editing and the new CRISPR technologies with their potential to alter our genetic makeup, to direct our evolution as a species, also asks serious questions about whether we have the necessary wisdom.

It also asks now that we can, what would we like to change? Some potential changes relate to health issues especially those with a clear genetic base. Others relate to identity and the things which define us such as the expression of sexuality or how we cope with disabilities. Modern Science has now given us the ability to direct the future evolution of ourselves and other living things. Synthetic DNA technologies which use letters (X, Y) beyond the four (G, T, C, A) which have resulted from evolutionary processes give the potential to produce radical new organisms.[4] In this book

---

4 King A (2020) 'Alien DNA' p. 25 in *Chemistry and Industry*, Issue 07/08.

I have attempted to explore such issues through chapters dealing explicitly with Covid19 and its impact (Chapter3), Climate Change (Chapter 10) and with one which continues the discussion which began at the Reformation, of the relationship between Science and Scripture (Chapter 2). There are chapters dealing with the potential outcomes (Chapters 5, 6 & 8) and societal consequences (Chapters 7 & 9) of Genome Editing.

Where and how to cover the underlying Science has been among the most difficult of decisions in bringing together this book. The Science Chapter with which I conclude (Chapter 12) began its life with its content distributed between the chapters, was then consolidated at the start of the book and has finished up at the end. There are good arguments for all of these placings, as colleagues who have kindly read earlier drafts of the script have commented. However, for those who wonder how we got here in scientific terms I conclude the book with the chapter which details the science journey which brought us to this point, perhaps as a different way of helping a reflection around where we go next.

Not For the First Time

In all of this there are useful questions we can ask such as, have we been here before and if so, what did we do then and what were the consequences? Unless you are over 600 years old you cannot really say our current experience of life with Covid19 is in the true sense *déjà vu*, but recorded history tells us that we have indeed been here before. Among the first known 'Plagues' was an outbreak of Influenza in Babylon in 1200 BCE. However, such reflections naturally take us back to one of the first well documented pandemics, the Black Death (Bubonic Plague caused by the bacteria *Yersinia pestis*) in the 14th century. The Black Death has been described as the plague which devastated a continent and destroyed a way of life. Churchill commented:

> A whole generation is slashed through by a hideous severance. The character of the pestilence was appalling. The disease itself stunned and for a time destroyed the life and faith of the world.[5]

By the end of 1346 there were rumours of a plague in the East which had devastated countries from India to Syria and which arrived in Sicily in late

---

5 Churchill WS (1969) 'The Century of Death', pp. 689-713 in *History of the English-Speaking Peoples*, Purnell, Bristol.

1347 and in England in 1348.The plague had moved along trade routes. The initial wave was followed by further waves in 1361-62 and 1369, 1371, 1379, 1390. The Black Death killed around 50 million people in Europe and perhaps as many as 200 million worldwide between 1346 and 1351 although cases were still being recorded until 1654. It occurred in a series of waves. Deaths represented around 60% of Europe's population. Around 80% of those infected died. It began in the black rat population, moved with the shipping trade while its spread was accentuated by the new developing trade links around Europe and from the Steppes region near the Caspian Sea. The only countries in Europe to be unaffected, Iceland and Finland, were those with minimal trade and hence less contact with others.

In 1720 there was a major outbreak in Marseille in France which killed around half of its population. The infection was brought in by ship and its incidence accelerated by official dithering and the involvement of local officials with a vested interest in the continuation of trade. Eventually the advance of the plague was stopped by a combination of trade embargoes, quarantines, the distribution of food aid and a disinfection campaign. This has considerable resonance with the impact of Covid19 where again too many Governments were slow to react because of the potential economic impact but ultimately adopted a policy of quarantine.

The current impact of Covid19 also parallels the outbreak of earlier *viral* diseases such as Polio (also known as Infantile Paralysis)[6] In the 1940's and 1950's it was responsible, worldwide, for around 600,000 deaths or cases of paralysis annually. Polio was a major cause of death in young people in the USA in the 1950's. Those who survived infection did so as a result of the use of an Iron Lung which took over the function of breathing for them in a related way to the modern ventilator. Many of those infected were symptomless, around a third experienced only a minor illness, while around 5% exhibited serious symptoms. In places where it was especially prevalent people quarantined themselves, public places were closed and social interaction was minimised. A cure for Polio falls within the period in which biological science developed

---

6 McRobbie LR (2020) The Man in the Iron Lung pp. 48-50 in *The Week* issue 1287, 11 July.

(Chapter12). It is thus part of our story.[7] It raises matters such as the interaction of individuals with the science process. Issues which develop our thinking.

Of a very different nature but helpfully related is the story of the people of Israel as recounted in Scripture. After the escape of the Israelites from Egypt they spent around 40 years journeying in the wilderness. During this time, they were living in tented accommodation with limited resources. The development of good hygiene practices was essential to survival. Some of these have survived as the distinctive hygiene practices detailed in Leviticus and still providing guidance to those of the Jewish faith. This has clear parallels with the current response to Covid19 and with its core set of hygiene measures such as hand washing and social distancing. During the period in the wilderness the people of Israel began to develop their distinctive faith, a series of attributes which distinguished them from other nations around them and which gave them identity. The Covid19 pandemic has led to the development of exceptionalism in a number of countries. In the UK we have seen claims for the development of our "world beating" app, ventilators and track and trace technologies!

The Bible as a whole gives not just an account of an increasing knowledge of God but also reflections about the evolving relationship between God and the world in which we live. Scripture can thus guide us as to how we ought to relate to God but also how we ought to interact with the world in which we find ourselves. Wisdom has ever been important. It is now needed as much as ever. Climate Change indicated that we were able to get things wrong on a global scale. Diseases in the past have been responsible for the total restructuring of society. The post Black Death World did not resemble what had gone before both in terms of social structures, how things were done and people's values. Covid provides a frighteningly similar parallel.

Whom is This Book For?

This Book came out of plans for a series of talks for Lent 2020. The talks themselves were a product of my five year period chairing the SEC's Church in Society Committee and the subjects discussed there. The aim was to bring into a period of reflection, consideration of the developments

---

7 See material on HeLa Cells, Polio Vaccines and Viruses in Chapter 12.

taking place in current biology and to question what might be their impact. The concept was driven by the potential impact of CRISPR, and related technologies, and their potential to change humanity as we have been. In the journey from a series of talks to a book there is a pilgrimage through the ideas which led to the original concept continuing but modified by all that has happened since the inception of the idea. When the idea for this book began, Climate Change was the predominant scientific issue being discussed on a global scale. 2019 had been the year of Extinction Rebellion. However, the disease Covid19 (caused by the virus SARS-CoV-2) entered global consciousness at the end of 2019 and by March 2020 it had come to dominate the news.

Embarking on any writing project raises the question What is its intended market? So, who is this book for? The simple answer is for anyone interested in the role of biological science in driving and forming the nature of society and for those interested in how faith-based traditions continue to be affected by society's pilgrimage through such issues. New developments in biology, such as Genome Editing, represent a paradigm shift. Is it a desirable direction of travel? Genome Editing has an ethical dimension, so the Science needs to be considered alongside sources such as Scripture. A hope is that together the new biology along with teaching from Scripture could provide an opportunity for people of faith to approach both in a different way. These issues are a real chance for churches to welcome the new developments while bringing its Wisdom tradition to bear and bringing God into the picture.

Finally

In a very real sense this book is a record of a personal journey in which I have been challenged to examine developments in Science which raise ethical and other 'would it be wise to' questions and to examine them against my Christian Faith. Usually the first step on such a journey is to formulate a question, the habitual response of Jesus, and to use that question as a vehicle for both exploration and discussion with others. That has led, in this book, to the use of the questions which have been part of my exploration which I hope that readers may find helpful in their pilgrimage through these issues.

Chapter 2

Science and Scripture, Two Ways or One?

The world we experience even on a day to day basis, extends beyond the physical, chemical, biological make-up of our planet. It has other dimensions. That the world *is*, is a mystery. All of this suggests that to understand 'what it means to be human' must extend beyond mere biology. Wider issues are significant for people of faith, but such contemplation is not restricted to them. It is important to examine the impact that advances in the biological sciences, especially those driven by CRISPR Genome Editing techniques and related approaches, might have on our humanity. Gene editing gives us the welcome potential to change some current medical disabilities. It also gives the potential to make changes to the human embryo so that the concept of 'designer babies' becomes a real possibility. Simply looking at developments as being either positive or negative seems inadequate. The question 'what it means to be human', as a core element within an approach to Science, is a key need of our time. That humanity *is*, is a mystery, but one worthy of exploration. Such an exploration for Christians will involve consideration of what is Science, and what is the nature of Scripture, as it is understood in our era.

So How Should we Understand Scripture?

Before looking at what Science is and its use in society, it seems wise to identify how Scripture is to be interpreted in this book – important so that both differences and common ground can be identified. Scripture is all too often misread. Many give it an authority and a literal status for which it was never intended. The Bible is not a single entity, but a library of books written at different times and usually arranged on the basis of subject links. Discussions of contemporary issues all too often seem to put it in opposition to what is described as a science led approach. This could happen in discussing Genome Editing and related matters.

In considering the role and impact of Scripture there are at least two major questions which impact upon its relationship with Science. The first of these is the impact of Scripture, and the Bible in particular, on how faith is currently practised i.e. what is commonly described as religion. This issue was recently addressed by John Barton,[8] who suggested

> that the Bible doesn't easily map onto particular approaches to faith or religious denominations. There are denominations which claim to be more closely founded on the Bible, but it is not always easy to see how their preaching or behaviour actually reflects the teaching of the Bible or even their own basis.

This inability to map easily prompts questions about the extent that Christianity can be seen as a faith based on a single book the Bible.

Judaism while reverencing Scripture is not Bible centred.

The Bible allows for constant interrogation and reinterpretation and so is fitted for a living faith.

Essentially religion, faith as it is currently practised, is impacted by more than what is in Scripture. Tradition and Reason are for many just as important. Tradition, practices which develop over time and result from interactions with the current cultural forces, is always important. Tradition can be expressed through ritual, liturgy and by the development of thinking about the nature of faith. Scripture is old but no older than other materials which impact our thinking. The oldest material in Scripture is thought to date to the eighth century BCE but with much material from the sixth century BCE and some from the second century BCE. Much of the Old Testament is thus more recent than Homer.

Reason, also a channel that the Holy Spirit uses, allows us to contribute insights from prayer, dialogue and life as it is being lived in particular places and times. Different approaches to faith tend to have a different balance of the elements - Scripture, Tradition and Reason. Many Protestant approaches would emphasise Scripture while more Catholic approaches would place more emphasis on Tradition. Liberal versions of either would place significant emphasis on Reason. Our current position is the result of a journey of almost two thousand years since the events described in Scripture. We have had that long to come to terms with Scripture and it continues to be a journey in which we remain engaged. For the past

---

8 Barton J (2019) 'Introduction: The Bible Today', pp. 1-17 in *A History of the Bible: The book and its faiths*, Allen Lane, London.

four hundred years or more, coming to terms with Science has been an important part of that adjustment.

The second issue, which occurs regardless of the mapping of Scripture and religion, is how Scripture is read and interpreted. For example, the Genesis accounts of the beginning of the world and the origin of life, which are discussed in more detail later, were never intended to be factual in our current understanding of that world. They do tell us much about the relationship between our world and our Creator, which is what it was always intended to do. Precise historical writing is a modern invention and represents a different literary genre. At its simplest Scripture can be understood as a story with a meaning, and one which has filled that role for many and over long periods of time and in very different cultural settings. Scripture has never needed to be future proofed, but our dynamic understanding of Scripture is a matter for continuing reflection. This is explored more fully in the section on the role of Scripture in a Scientific World later in this chapter.

Today we live in a world which prides itself on being dominated by fact and by evidence. The provision of real-time 24hr News Channels have accentuated this approach to life. The basis of modern existence seems predicated on the possession of facts (News) and possessions (Consumerism)! Not being 'evidence-based' is a problem and a challenge for the church today. It is not possible for faith to become 'evidence based' in a conventional sense. Testimony, the experience of those with faith, collectively supports the view that faith remains alive and helps engagement with the current world. This requires that Scripture is understood for what it is and not in ways for which it was not intended. This framework has implications for the use of Scripture in respect of the issues at the core of this book. Before visiting more specific issues about Scripture it seems appropriate to consider in a parallel way to the above, what Science is and is not.

The Nature and Role of Science

If the above material gives an understanding of how Scripture is seen in the writing of this book it is important to ask similar questions of Science. How should Science be seen? The definition of Science given by the OED is complex with 5 separate options as to how the word may be understood. The options most relevant to our discussion are:

- A branch of study which is either concerned with a connected body of demonstrated truths or with observed facts systematically classified and more or less colligated by being brought under general laws and which includes trustworthy methods for the discovery of new truths.

- A particular branch of knowledge, an occupation, needing trained skills.

This implies that defining Science is not simple. It emphasises the need for skills, facts and the bringing together and discussion of observations. Its out-working in society, the technologies to which it gives rise, can differ from its underlying philosophical base. Clearly Science is an approach to ordering the world. It often has a distinct language which can result in differences in the meaning of words relative to their use in standard conversation. An example of this is the word 'theory'. In ordinary conversation it commonly describes a speculation. In Science it's a conceptual framework bringing together current information. The concept of the electron is a theory. The concept of evolution is a theory. The concept of the gene is a theory. All Science is based on theories e.g. chemistry on matter being made of atoms, physics on quantum mechanics and relativity, geology on plate tectonics, and biology on evolution.[9]

The disparity in the use of language between scientists and others suggests there is scope for misunderstandings. In Science proof is not an applicable concept. Scientific conclusions are never certain – everything is provisional. Uncertainty, provisionality and change are key elements and the reason why scientists disagree. Being aware of this is important in considering the subjects discussed in this book. The consequences of a popular misunderstanding of science have been explored by Tom McLeish[10] in the form of a contemporary parable. The world as we know it can be explained in very different ways, as a result of applying different philosophical concepts. The terms 'Supernaturalism' and 'Naturalism' have been suggested as identifiers for alternative ways of explaining the world.[11] Such a classification is simplistic but because the distinction is commonly used, I explore it here. For some this division seems logical but it assumes

9 Ellis J (2010) *How Science Works: Evolution,* Springer, Dordrecht.

10 McLeish T (2014) Introduction pp. 1-5 in *Faith and Wisdom in Science,* OUP.

11 Ellis J (2010) Two ways of explaining the world pp. 1-5 in *How Science Works: Evolution.*

a clear distinction, which often is misleading and frequently is divisive. Its common use suggests the need to explore both the separation this leads to but also what might be the value of a more unifying concept.

'Supernaturalism' asserts that alongside the physical world in which we exist there co-exists another presence which is 'invisible', the entity we call God. The invisible agent can interact with the physical world. All human cultures throughout history have produced such beliefs. The concept of belief, a statement of faith which is independent of being testable by the scientific method, is at the heart of this approach to life.

'Naturalism' refers to a physical world which most commonly behaves according to unvarying regularities as determined by observation and experiment, 'the laws of nature'. Built into it is an assumption that natural events will have natural causes. The methodological testing of ideas is important to the testing of theories. Scientific knowledge is always provisional rather than certain, and indeed (like Supernaturalism) contains a very real element of uncertainty and faith.

In her description of the development of the CRISPR technology, Jenifer Doudna relates the many ways in which the underlying theory changed in the light of the new information which came from an increasingly wide range of experiments.[12] There were many disagreements. Nothing gets proved! This is particularly true for biology where so much is probabilistic rather than deterministic. Science is how we test 'Naturalism'. It is a set of ideas derived from the best evidence available, based on reason, applied to data and always open to change. Its key concepts include theory, hypothesis and fact. A fact is the result of an observation or an experiment. Hypotheses are testable speculations which might explain facts. Theories are coherent conceptual models that explain sets of facts. An understanding of Science is needed to assess the role which Genome Editing may have, the effects of the SARS-CoV-2 virus and the probable impact of Climate Change.

That particular individuals follow elements of the above philosophical approaches to seeing the world is not disputed. Different people have followed one or other, or both of these two approaches.[13] Can they exist in parallel? Christians who are scientists, knowing that God has made the

---

12 Doudna J and Sternberg SH (2017) *A Crack in Creation*, Bodley Head, London.

13 The non-overlapping 'Magisterium' of Stephen Gould and the parallel epistemologies of John Polkinghorne are examples of this.

world with its own marvellous life to be explored, share with other scientists the same methods of exploration. The real debate is whether 'naturalism' is a total explanation of life without mention of God, or whether God sustains nature and works through it, but remains unseen.

With your strong arm you rescued your people . . . your path was through the sea . . . and none could mark your footsteps.[14]

But that is a debate about philosophy or worldview, not about science. Religious scientists would not introduce supernatural explanations into their science but use the approaches in parallel. Tom McLeish spells out how this can work. A unified approach needs explanations which can link and hence the need for a theology of science. This would place science within a larger narrative, which involves elements such as creation and healing, and places the values and purpose of humanity within a wider setting than would be given by science alone. The simplifying terms of *'Naturalism'* and *'Supernaturalism'* or *Theology and Science* both include the word 'and', which emphasises a division. Nevertheless, many find such distinctions helpful when applied to different questions or in different contexts within the same issue, and in discussions with wider audiences.[15] A scientist can employ critical realism.[16] As explored above, scientific knowledge has emphasised that the Bible contains materials which should be read as a story with purpose.[17]

However, like changes in the meaning of words when they become part of everyday conversation, understanding of the role of Science changes when it moves into public debate. Claims made during public debates around contentious subjects, such as in the Genetic Modification (GM) era,[18] impacted public confidence. During that debate Government argued

---

14 Psalm 77: 19.

15 McLeish T (2014) 'A theology of Science' pp. 166-172 in *Faith and Wisdom in Science.*

16 Priest E (2015) 'Introduction – has science made Christianity redundant?' pp. 1-12 in *Towards an Integration of Science and Theology?* Grosvenor Essay 11, SEC, Edinburgh.

17 Barton J (2019) 'The Bible and Science' pp. 427-429 in *A History of the Bible: The book and its faiths*, Allen Lane, London.

18 See material on Genetic Modification in Chapter 12.

that policy should always be science led. In the Covid19 era we have heard the same mantra repeated at Government Press conferences. This asks again whether Science really can lead to a single view which can then become the unique driver. The mantra of policy simply following Science has protected the advocates of policies from the questioning of outcomes. It's important to ask how much of the modern 'Science' used in the media, where claims of Science providing 'proof' are commonly made, strictly follows the scientific method? How much of what is detailed as Science is actually engineering or technology which have their roots in Science, assume that scientific theories are sufficiently certain to permit their practical application but are not strictly 'Science'? So can Scripture, as explored above, and Science be compatible and work together to give a more nuanced picture? One of the basic premises of this book is that they can and that it's helpful when they do. It is also assumed that in so doing we add to our journey of understanding the out-working of God's purposes in our world.

The Role of Scripture in a Scientific World

Can Scripture be read as compatible with developments in Science? Can Science become an integral part of both the interpretation of Scripture and the modern faith journey? How does such a voice become relevant to society as a whole? How can sacred texts help to put new developments into the context of faith? How can the most general of ethical principles from Scripture be of help in response to specific questions?[19]

As discussed earlier the major Abrahamic religious Scriptures contain different literary forms. They describe the interactions between God and the People of Israel over a period of more than a thousand years. It describes this through what might now be called a Case Study, centred on the people of Israel and on the ways in which their interactions with God led them to develop both an understanding of the world as they found it and of the purpose of life. In recording this journey, the compilers of the Bible included material from a range of literary forms. They included stories, prophecy, poetry, instructions, all of which it was thought had been either inspired by God or represented guidance from God. The material in the Scriptures was designed to communicate, to inform and to provide information which is memorable. The Wisdom Literature is of particular

---

19 Thomson M (2005) *Ethical Theory*, Hodder Murray, London.

interest.[20] Wisdom literature is not unique to the Bible.[21] The people in Israel who were responsible for the Hebrew Scriptures borrowed from the people around them. Collections of proverbs, which can be dated to before 2,000 BC are known to have existed in Sumeria and in Babylon. Some of what we read in Proverbs and in Job can be found in Sumerian and Assyrian literature. Much also came from Egypt. The international nature of this literary form suggests why it continues to have value. It is designed to help us think about difficult questions. In the Wisdom Literature[22] there are specifically directed statements in some of the Psalms. There is advice in Proverbs and Ecclesiastes, as there is outside the Old Testament in the wisdom of Sirach. Help is given in story form in Job.[23]

Why should people of faith be interested in the novel areas of Science that we describe in this book? How might such changes impact our relationship with God? How do issues, such as the possibility of genome-edited children being produced, with changes aimed at enhancing human properties, link to our vision of humanity within God's creation, as set out in the opening to John's Gospel.[24] Jesus called us to be in the world and to take out his message to those in the world.

The impact of the moral teaching of Scripture remains, even for many who reject the existence of God. For those with a faith it remains a record of a developing understanding and intimacy between God and humanity. For Christians, the New Testament represents a paradigm shift in the development of that relationship. The story has however continued both through the development of tradition which has a key role in how faith is practised and in the continuing practice of the re-interpretation of Biblical texts. Increasing quantities of scientific knowledge, particularly about the start of the universe and the origin of life, have challenged and enhanced our reading of traditional texts.

---

20 Explicit advice on how to behave which is found in Biblical books such as Proverbs, Job, Ecclesiastes and Sirach.

21 Boadt L (1997) 'The International World of Wisdom', pp. 12-13 in *The Book of Job*, [now] Lion Hudson, Oxford.

22 Barton J (2019) 'Law and Wisdom' pp. 60-88.

23 McLeish (2014) 'At the Summit: the Book of Job', pp. 102-148 in *Faith and Wisdom in Science*, OUP.

24 John 1: 2-4.

There is however no direct guidance about the use of technologies such as Genome Editing! There is considerable emphasis on the nature of what are commonly termed 'miracles'. The 'miracles' carried out by Jesus suggest the importance of the faith of the person being healed.[25] The remarkable achievements of modern medicine lead us to ask the question 'What would we now regard as being a miracle?' Does the miraculous have to be totally inexplicable or can the actions of people, such as those who treat patients with serious illnesses, be part of a miracle? Does God act by inspiring the right people in the right place at the right time? It matters that the church focuses upon and answers the questions of today and not those of an earlier era.[26] A continuing issue is what can be read as *literal* and what needs to be interpreted as *metaphor*.

The following subject areas have been selected as being both those which have led to debate between the church and the scientific community and which are critical to the issues discussed in this book. It's appropriate to begin with creation because if we accept that life as we know it resulted from evolution then we, humanity, share a common heritage with all life.

Creation.[27]   Genesis, the first book of the Bible, begins with an account of the creation of the universe and of the earth.[28] Coming at the beginning of both the Hebrew Scriptures and the Christian Bible immediately it provides us with a challenge as to how we will engage with all that follows. In his commentary on the Book of Genesis John Hargreaves suggests that passages from Genesis need to be approached as we might the singing of a hymn and seen wholly in the context of praising God. Seen in this way many confusions evaporate.[29]

In popular dialogue the essential questions have resolved into was the universe created as described and less than 10,000 years ago and were all living things created at the same time or are there other more realistic interpretations? If a literal reading is regarded as non-prescriptive

---

25 Mark 2: 3-5.

26 Spong JS (2018) *Unbelievable*, Harper, New York.

27 These issues are discussed more fully under Evolution in Chapter 12.

28 Genesis 1: 1-2, 3.

29 Hargreaves J (1969) *A Guide to the Book of Genesis*, TEF Study Guides 3, SPCK, London.

then there is no insurmountable incompatibility between Scripture and the Big Bang Theory of astrophysics. Scripture is clear that God had a major role in Creation, but the mechanism is not spelt out. Similarly, a literal reading could suggest all living things appearing in their current form. Darwinism, the theory that things evolved from a starting point by natural selection to where we are now, provides an alternative view. For those Christians who accept Scripture as a metaphor alongside the Darwinian view i.e. who can reconcile Naturalism and Supernaturalism as co-existing, they are compatible. Evolution does not have to displace God from Creation.[30] As both a scientist and a priest, for me the question of what preceded the Big Bang remains a matter of faith.

Adam and Eve.[31] Did humanity evolve in a way similar to the rest of life or did it arise spontaneously? A literal reading of Genesis 2: 4 – 3: 24 would suggest that all humanity came from a single individual. Genetics tells us that this cannot be so. Again, John Hargreaves suggests that had the compilers of Genesis wanted to give a clear factual story then it would have been presented as a single narrative. However, by using the technique of telling various stories the text becomes more memorable and helps us to focus on God and man's relationship with God.

As discussed above, evolution can sit with a metaphorical interpretation of Scripture. The origins of humanity can be understood as an output of evolutionary change. As with the issues at the heart of creation interpreting human origin in this way returns us to being rooted unequivocally among all living things and so gives an added context to the new ability to modify the genome. This change in thinking also has a wider significance in relation to both hierarchy and power within society. How this section of Scripture is interpreted has had a significant impact on the roles and status within society of the two sexes. [Some people are certain Adam was only the prototype – Eve is the real deal!]

Gender.[32] Traditional views of a binary divide within society between male and female have resulted in a view that all must fall into one of

---

30 See under Evolution in Chapter 12.

31 See Greenblatt S (2017) *The Rise and Fall of Adam and Eve*, Bodley Head, London.

32 Some of the scientific issues related to this are discussed within the section on Epigenetics in Chapter 12.

these categories and that any deviation from this is a 'life-style choice'. Although the subject is mentioned in Leviticus[33] and briefly elsewhere in the Bible, a very real question is why this one issue has been considered to be quite so important. We are all defined as individuals by a range of characteristics and by the things we have done. Why for some has sexuality been so important in defining who we are? Views of this type have resulted in a particular view of homosexuality and are the basis of current disagreements over same-gender marriage. Earlier in this Chapter I discussed the role of tradition in placing particular emphasis on particular verses of Scripture. This is a potent example of the consequences of such an approach. The existence of people with an ill-defined physical sexual expression has long questioned the binary understanding. Better understanding of genetics and epigenetics reinforce the concept of a continuum with distinct variations and not a binary division.

Food. Food[34] is among the most common topics discussed in Scripture.[35] Food linked issues dominate the Hebrew Scriptures. Food and the related food production, agriculture, provide the basis for many of the parables recounted by Jesus.[36] Scripture seems clear that the production of food is linked to issues which go far beyond how much might be produced from an area of land. How this is done, who does it, how it is prepared and how it is shared out are critical. In how we produce, honour and share our food are the foundations of societal interactions. It informs our treatment of the Earth, our relationships with other living things and how we should trade with others. The final meeting of Jesus with his disciples is centred around a meal of fish.[37] The relationship between humanity and God is seen in relation to food as being at the heart of something vital to life.

---

33 Leviticus 18: 22.

34 Some of the scientific issues related to food are discussed in the section on GM in Chapter 12.

35 Exodus 16: 2-36 represents the first major mention. Leviticus 1 begins guidance on the treatment of food.

36 Matthew 12 begins a block of food production teaching.

37 John 21: 4-13.

Healing. Healing[38] is among the most common topics in the New Testament.[39] Jesus is identified with a wide range of acts of healing. Healing and health are important issues for Christians. We are told that Jesus healed people with a range of health conditions: diseases e.g. leprosy, illnesses e.g. uncontrolled bleeding, and mental health conditions e.g. possession. Many of these events are commonly described as being miracles. We are not told how Jesus did this, what was the nature of the healing nor what were the consequences of the healing for the life of the person receiving it. It is commonly assumed that the person was completely restored to a normal life rather than being enabled to cope with life. This issue is at the heart of discussions around disability and of whether the new technologies which are the basis of this book ought to be used as a means of moving everyone towards a 'set normal' rather than being encouraged and helped to adapt to a variety of ways of experiencing the challenges of life living with disability. It also prompts us to consider what we might identify as a miracle in today's society.

Disease. Disease is related to health but gets a lesser mention in Scripture. Diseases can be life threatening to both humans and animals. Many of the rules detailed in Leviticus are designed to provide means of disease control and management[40] and have had a role at crucial points in the Bible story. Similar matters have had an important role in our time as a result of the impact of Covid19. The diseases which affected animals and the first born of Egypt were important to the people of Israel being released from slavery in Egypt[41] Leprosy features in both the story of Elisha[42] and is the focus of several of Jesus' healings.[43] Leprosy was not immediately life threatening but it resulted in social isolation, lepers were outcasts from society. This has a clear resonance with the same disease in our current world and with the impact of many other diseases.

---

38 Material relevant to healing is covered in Chapter 12, on HeLa Cells, Polio, Vaccines, CRISPR (see also Glossary).

39 Matthew 8 begins a recounting of the first of Jesus healing miracles.

40 Leviticus 12: 1-5.

41 Exodus 9: 1-21, 11: 1-10.

42 2 Kings 5: 1-19.

43 Luke 17: 11-19.

End of life. For all of us Death is a certainty. Perhaps because it is and always has been such a certainty, it receives little coverage in Scripture other than in relation to the importance of the next life and a role in the Kingdom of Heaven. Accounts of individuals brought back from the dead such as the story of Lazarus provide material for reflection.[44] This can lead to a view of this life being of little importance compared with what is to come. This can comfort and help to prepare for the end of life but it may not help accept the issues of ageing and the progressive loss of health, and with many of the decisions which may need to be made.

Have we been here before?

The Lockdown has given us all more time to read and to look at books in our personal libraries which have remained unvisited for some time. One of the books I re-discovered was the one arising from the 1970's Institute of Biology Symposium entitled *The Future of Man*.[45] A group of scientists, had come together to discuss the ethical and political implications of scientific discoveries. Among the topics discussed were the right to reproduce, the artificial synthesis of new life forms and how to keep people alive. Some issues just continue to be important. All are as significant now as they were in 1971. It is important to note that some questions and issues seem to be perennial and that others merely keep re-appearing in a new guise.

In discussing the issues around In Vitro Fertilisation (IVF) one of the editors of that 1970's volume[46] commented that egg transfer, what we now call IVF, could be regarded as dangerous as well as potentially beneficial. It impacts something which for most is personal and even emotional. Were it to have economic or political motives then it would be unacceptable. In commenting on issues related to ageing he suggests that while preserving human life long after breeding potential has passed seemed generally desirable, it didn't immediately seem to confer a selective advantage. However, in human society it may help the structure and function of families and society as a whole. Keeping alive those with chronic illnesses poses rather different questions and ones where the interests of society and the individual may be very different.

---

44 John 11: 1-43.

45 Ebling FJ and Heath GW (1971) *The Future of Man*, Academic Press, London.

46 Ebling FJ (1972) 'Introduction', pp. xiii-xviii, *ibid*.

So Where Do We End?

Any attempt to discuss how issues in the biological and medical sciences relate to issues of faith will not be breaking wholly new ground.[47] I am conscious that I am following in many sets of earlier footsteps. In my attempts to develop links between Scripture and the issues of modern biology I have followed two distinct approaches. Both Science and Scripture make use of stories. First, identifying a real person as the basis of a case study exemplifies and personifies the issue. Second, identifying a person from within the Hebrew Scriptures will, I hope, provide a scriptural insight into the issues and follow the approach of the Wisdom tradition. The aim is for the use of real people and figures from Scripture to make the material memorable.

---

47 Wyatt J (2009) *Matters of Life and Death, Human dilemmas in the light of Christian faith*, Inter Varsity Press, London.

Chapter 3

COVID19 and all that

This chapter opens with a piece written by Margaret in the early days of Lockdown as we discussed and reflected on the impact of Covid 19 on all our lives. Margaret writes:

In the late 80s early 90s I was employed in various areas of Health Education and at one period during that time my work focussed on AIDS Education. I was fortunate to be selected to attend a week-long European Conference on AIDS, hosted in Sweden by the Swedish Health Authorities, exploring issues surrounding this new epidemic caused by a virus – the Human Immunodeficiency Virus – which became known as HIV and against which to this day there is still no effective vaccine.

As we reeled from the shock of the Corona Virus, which became known as Covid 19, spreading rapidly and seemingly uncontrollably westwards from China – I was struck by the coincidences and backstories of the AIDS epidemic and the Covid 19 Pandemic

1980 and 2020[48] – forty years apart, but inextricably linked in the eyes of future historians by these words 'BEFORE and AFTER the VIRUS'.

When we come to look back on life living alongside the Covid19 virus, whenever that is, there will no doubt be many definitive books documenting and chronicling the effects, the problems, the organisational deficits, the government's shortcomings, the societal effects, and the fears and uncertainties we experienced. Things will have changed. Life will have changed. There will be feelings of life before and after THE VIRUS. That is where there are such strong parallels between 1980 and 2020. One such book written in the 1980s – *And The Band Played On* by Randy Shilts[49] – about the HIV virus, compares that pandemic to a war dividing time, memories and life into before and after for all those who lived through it.

---

48 Reflection by Margaret Hadley. Reflection composed in the early days of the infection in the UK.
49 Shilts R (1987) *And The Band Played On*, St Martin's Press, USA.

A defining moment for society, values and behaviour. He calls the before a time of innocence, excess and idealism, and a time before Death.

The common link is the invisible threat of a virus – in fact two different viruses but their world-wide impact, their lack of discrimination whilst at the same time exhibiting adverse selectivity, the confusion and mishandling of their spread and to date there being no effective protection against them in the form of a vaccine, show uncanny similarities in approach and societal outcomes.

1980. The disease as yet undefined which was later named AIDS (Acquired Immune Deficiency Syndrome) had been around since the early 70s but manifested a variety of seemingly oddly unconnected symptoms which were a puzzle to the medical profession around the world. As research progressed it became clear that it was confined originally to a particular sector of society – Gay men – and as such, in the way of the times, was not rated as high priority and, even worse, attracted opprobrium rather than empathy. In America, the disease hot-spot at the time, there was a long history of discrimination in terms of a lack of rights, opportunities and healthcare for Gay people and against which the Gay community had been fighting and gradually had been making an impact thanks to a small group of influential people. Down the years there had been marches, protests, riots but above all a plea for the Gay community to be treated with equal regard first and foremost as human beings.

In 1980 The Gay Freedom Day Parade was a pivotal moment with 30,000 people grouped in 240 contingents marching through downtown San Francisco watched by 200,00 spectators. A lot of people.

However, the world was slow to react. There would be still a long journey ahead politically, medically and economically before the virus which caused the disease and its life-changing effects was understood and accepted.

2020. As the year turned, what up till then had been obscure and confused anecdotes emanating from a little-known place in China called Wuhan, became corroboration that a new virus was rampant. It presented with seemingly oddly unconnected pneumonia type symptoms, indiscriminate in its attack whilst at the same time selectively fatal for older people, and extremely contagious and infectious.

At first the attempts by individual Chinese medics to raise the alarm and awareness of this unusual disease, in the Autumn of 2019, were thwarted. This appeared to be an unknown virus which spread very rapidly. Through television screens the rest of the world watched nightly scenes more reminiscent of horror movies as team after team of masked and gowned doctors and nurses fought desperately but unsuccessfully to halt the ever-increasing death rate and contain the spread of the virus. It was subsequently recognised as a Corona virus and known as Covid19.

LOCKDOWN[50]

Lockdown a funny word   Not used much before
Heard it first in Wuhan   Far away Wuhan
Deserted eerie streets   Inflatable looking men in masks
Hosing streets   Serious looking medics in masks
Treating dying people
The virus spread   Lockdown spread
Like a ghost they crept silently stealthily   From East to West
Now they're here   Lockdown's strange   Life is strange
Choice is gone but not gone
If we don't choose Lockdown   We could be gone

'Lockdown' became a new everyday term as first China then other Asian countries, followed by European ones, tried to contain the fatal spread by literally locking-down cities, towns and people for long periods. The long journey through this pandemic still stretches ahead. A proven vaccine still eludes the researchers, the excess death rates persist, the disproportionate effect on BAME (Black Asian Minority Ethnic) communities remains unclear. There are also parallels of tardiness of government and health organisations' reaction, conflicting scientific advice, and increasing awareness of inequalities requiring long overdue action. Above all, in both cases, life before and after will never be the same again.

There can barely have been a time when our awareness of the fragility of life, reflections about identity and the asking of the question 'what does it means to be human?' have come into such sharp focus as in the early months of 2020. Right from the moment on 23rd March 2020 when the UK prime Minister announced a National Lockdown it was clear that life would never be as it had been at the onset of the year. A new paradigm for life as it would now be was in the process of being established.

---

50 Unpublished Poem written by Margaret Hadley.

Finally these words formulated themselves in my head as I walked around my neighbourhood in early Spring – a new take on the concept of '2020 Vision' !

2020 VISION[51]

Silence everywhere
Almost dead silence
Dead streets lined with dead cars
It's Apocalyptical
Nothing moves
Save the daffodils nodding gently in the breeze
Where are all the people?
Lone strangers cross the street as you approach
It was nothing you said!
In fact, nothing much is being said
The weirdness of the new reality
Social isolation the new norm
Wide awareness of a metric measurement
The new 'INGS' are here
ShieldING QueuING DeliverING ClappING
LivING's not as we know it
But we who have life are the lucky ones
There's thousands of dead in the silence

Following on from that. With a book which principally is an evaluation of Genome Editing and related issues, why include a chapter on a viral disease Covid19? Covid19 has dominated media coverage for most of 2020. It has wiped from television news almost every other issue, including Brexit and Climate Change which were ubiquitous in the news in 2019. It seems therefore inappropriate to avoid it. Covid19 is resulting in major changes to so much of how life is lived and to both individual and societal concerns. It seems probable that the virus causing Covid19 will impact on both the extent to which Genome Editing is used and how it is used. Serendipity maybe, but the first use of Genome Editing on a human embryo brought to term (Chapter 5) was to give enhanced resistance to a virus! Covid19 also emphasises in a way which has perhaps not been

---

51 Unpublished poem by Margaret Hadley.

so clear since the advent of Spanish Flu in the early years of the twentieth century or the Black Death in the fourteenth century, the ways in which a single disease can lead to a total change to the values and functioning of societies across the globe. Essentially Covid19 has led to a major rethink about what is important in life – the issues which make up the heart of this book.

An advertisement for a charity in a recent issue of New Scientist said:

> Far from being a great leveller the coronavirus crisis highlights societies' deep-rooted inequalities.[52]

Who is impacted and how, are always important? While all in the population are potentially infectable by Covid19 it is clear that deaths have been mainly among those over 70, especially where they had pre-existing health issues, and in those from the BAME communities. This re-raises the issues of the Atlas of Death[53] debate of the early 1980's, which are discussed in Chapter 9. That study emphasised that life expectancy varied between occupations and across the UK. The emerging story of Covid19 shows the role of political decisions in the handling of the issues on the impact of a novel disease and thus the human role in the resulting effects of pandemics.[54]

Continuing this Story

As highlighted above, outbreaks of serious diseases have long had a major role in shaping the world. In the opening chapter and later in this chapter I reflect on the impact of the Black Death in the fourteenth Century. The advent of the Corona virus, Covid19 has had a truly global impact. It has been the first challenge to the global social structures which have evolved since the middle of the 20th century. Covid19 represents the first occasion when the people of our generations have had to come to terms with their lives being shaped by a force completely outwith their control. Death and illness have been repositioned, as major considerations within the nature of human confidence. Once again human beings have

---

52 Barnardo's advertisement (2020) 'Signal Boost', p. 23 in *New Scientist*, 6th June 2020.

53 Pearson H (2016) *The Life Project*, pp. 172-173, Allen Lane, London.

54 Vaughan A (2020) 'How it all went wrong in the UK', pp. 8-9 in *New Scientist*, 6th June 2020.

been reminded of mortality and that human life is unequivocally finite (a theme further reflected on in Chapter 9). In addition, this has impacted on everyone. Being financially well off has not provided a 'get out of jail card' nor the need not to worry.

Possibilities. Science Fiction novels foresee the world populated with people who have greater strength or higher intelligence. Up to now these 'aspirations' have been confined to Science Fiction. However, advances in Genome Editing and the new CRISPR technologies caused us to consider, for the first time ever, how we might like to change the genetic code which makes us what we are. This was the situation in Autumn 2019 when work on this book began. Yes, there would be a need to reflect on how these new possibilities might be used, questions as to whether it might help in mitigating the impact of Climate Change but essentially Genome Editing was more evidence of humanity being able to control the future.[55] The arrival of the Covid19 virus changed all of this.

And Consequences. So how did life change as a result of the advent of this virus? There were major effects on all of the following which formerly made up the foundations of life as it was.

a) How we viewed the world and the role and the related consequences of global trade and travel. Things which we previously regarded as major benefits such as the easy ability to holiday in exotic overseas places, inexpensive clothing from the developing world and competitively priced electrical goods from China and Korea suddenly were viewed in a very different way. Overseas holidays became difficult as a result of a need to quarantine if returning from particular overseas destinations and with affected destinations announced at short notice.

b) Within the world as we now found it, perspectives on the centrality of employment as the universal source of income and as the largest single driver of how society is organised and a total obligation for all who were able, changed. Suddenly employment seemed less important. It became something which could be done from home. This change alone impacted many of the 'support-service' businesses e.g. sandwich bars, which had developed to support working away from home. However once past the peak of infections and on the road to a new normality, employment and

---

55 Carey N (2020) *Hacking the Code of Life: How Gene Editing Will Rewrite our Futures*, Icon Books, London.

the economy resumed the driving seat. Working from home again became undesirable particularly in the eyes of Government.

c) In a very fundamental way our perspectives on the importance of contact and communication with other people both in our families and our social circles were forced to change. Lockdown, being required to remain in your own home, as a component of social distancing, deprived grandparents of family links and everyone of face-to-face contact for long periods. Digital technologies helped but identified real gaps in the process of total communication. The accompanying sense of isolation had perhaps the greatest impact on those over the age of 70 and those who were classed as vulnerable and so subject to more restrictions than other groups. Also, as the months have passed, the restriction of social contact has shown to have had a significant negative impact on the mental health of many young people.

d) The importance of choice and the ability to make decisions over how we used our time and where we could go- just went! - and consequently allowed society to identify which things really mattered to life and which we were able to do without. Some of these decisions were to have significant implications for employment e.g. the hospitality industry

e) How we prioritised the absolute importance and value of different occupations. Which were critical to the most important areas of life and which were only vital to life as we had previously constructed it? Some formerly highly paid jobs, such as those in the City, no longer seemed to be quite so vital. Other less well-regarded jobs such as waste disposal workers, supermarket till operators and care home staff all now seemed that much more important.

f) Our confidence in dealing with the problems and issues of life and our certainty in our ability to both take decisions and to cope with risk were impacted. This has perhaps been among the single largest effects. Before Covid19 we lived in a confident world which we believed was under our control, most of the time. Suddenly we were less clear about the wisdom of even minor decisions e.g. should we go out to a shop. We were concerned about risk. We sought assurances that particular choices would not involve risk. We needed clarity in relation to the risks involved in an action we took both for ourselves and for others. This was perhaps most visible in relation to the use of internet shopping. For many it had been their norm pre-Covid19 but during and even after the end of Lockdown it came to dominate the retail sector even for the over 70s. For many years before Covid19 the John Lewis chain had used the slogan 'Never knowingly undersold'. Schlepping around stores had come to an end. The move of much of its business on-line ended the slogan's use and validity, a potent symbol of how life was now going to be lived.

g) How priorities within healthcare were ranked – essentially the priority given to dealing with cases of Coronavirus compared to that assigned to other health issues such as the treatment of cancers or to IVF. Among the most significant of questions became how we now viewed the priorities accorded to people of different ages and with different health histories?

h) General priorities. How ought we to rank the importance of education compared to particular sectors of commerce like the Pub trade. How did we equate previous societal priorities such as maintaining traditional standards and expectations in relation to national examinations with the need to be fair to individuals and within a wholly unprecedented situation, how to assign grades to students in the absence of examinations? Issues around examination grades seem likely to result in radical changes to both how education is delivered and assessed.

i) The role played by Science in decision making within Government and its stated use as the absolute driver of all decisions on all aspects of the Government's approach to dealing with the pandemic. The science content of media coverage of Covid19 increased , with people being introduced to new concepts such as 'R' numbers and some university scientists becoming television personalities. As part of this, greater priority has been given to the developing of the technology to make things such as ventilators, protective clothing, vaccines and testing facilities within the UK, apparently above all other economic aims.

All of these have modified how we now regard the key issues which previously we saw as being important – and all because of a virus.

Viruses. What are viruses? Where do viruses fit into a life spectrum? Viruses are found wherever there is life but have no fossil record. We have long been conscious of disease-causing bacteria, such as those responsible for TB, Cholera and Anthrax. Many/most of these have been brought under control with the use of antibiotics. Other equally serious diseases such as Smallpox, Measles, Flu remained both relatively unexplained and resistant to treatment. Some were reduced in impact through vaccination. A detailed description of both viruses in general and of Covid19 are provided in Chapter 12 but their principal characteristics are briefly reviewed here.

By the 1920s we were clear that a range of viruses existed and were the cause of diseases such as the Spanish Flu. Since 2002 two new coronaviruses that can infect humans and result in more severe disease have appeared. They are transmitted primarily via droplets in coughs and sneezes. On 31st December 2019, Chinese authorities notified the World Health Organisation of an outbreak of viral pneumonia in Wuhan City. On 10th February, the WHO named the disease caused by the novel coronavirus SARS-CoV-2, COVID-19. Coronaviruses have spiked proteins on their surface which fit into receptors already present on the surface of a human cell which then allows them to enter the cell. Studies of the virus causing Covid19, found it to be particularly aggressive which permitted it to spread easily from person to person. It is believed that the basic reproductive number (R) of COVID19 – i.e. the number of new cases generated by each infected person – is between 2.0 and 3.0, and so higher than Influenza (1.3).

The New Questions. Covid19 posed many questions and raised a number of issues – some were international, others related to the decisions of national governments. Fundamentally we questioned what was truly essential and what was a societal led add-on. Maslow's hierarchy of needs was revisited. Governments across the world limited freedoms. Most prioritised control or elimination of the virus over business issues. Work became limited to essential activities which were dominated by health care, the supply of food, communication (including posted, spoken and visual media), transport for essential workers and basic services such as the collection of waste. Some things which used to happen continued, but in a new form. Many found that they were able to work from home using digital technologies. Similar technologies allowed parts of the retail trade to continue, while large amounts of education were delivered using digital approaches. It is interesting to ask could we have coped or how different might the approach have been without digital communication? A range of societal trends came together to produce major changes. Mobile phones continued to expand their role in the provision of information. 'Just in time', a business concept which eliminated the need for every business to 'pre-store' all their needs, increased its role in relation to information. Information could be browsed for and acquired on a 'just in time' basis leading to a group who could be termed TISIGs (The Instant Screen Info Generation).

Many things went – the most substantial being contact with others. Being human, for most, involves being in community, at the least with close friends and families. In addition, the provision of health care became a key issue. Covid19 questioned whether there was need to ration healthcare provision which previously had seemed unthinkable. Decisions as to who should get or not get resources became a live issue. This was discussed on the BBC 'Sunday am' religious programme – the issue was whether it was appropriate to focus resources on those most likely to survive. This would have focused limited resources on younger healthy patients and a presumption against treating older patients and those with underlying health issues. The alternative would have been to focus on the needs of all individuals with no presumed assumptions. Conflicts emerged in respect of potential shortages of ventilators, limitations to the number of available tests for the presence of the virus, the availability of intensive care beds and adequate supplies of PPE.

It re-opened the issues raised by the novelist GB Shaw in his book *The Doctor's Dilemma*. We were reminded of long-standing ill-health issues (discussed in Chapter 9), which could result in some being considered as 'less important' where a choice was needed. Similarly, being over the age of 70 years negatively impacted access to health care and a push for vulnerable groups to accept DNRs (Do Not Resuscitate classifications) Older people were transferred from the NHS to Care facilities so as to free up space. That this occurred without appropriate testing, PPE and hygiene measures resulted in a significant number of deaths. In themselves this identifies society's priorities.

A Case Study?

In the other chapters of this book individual people who provide an exemplar of the development being discussed have been selected. Across the world and within Europe so many people had died as a result of infection with the virus that singling out any one individual seemed inappropriate. There is however a pattern to many of the deaths. Susceptibility has been greatest among:

- Those over the age of 70
- Males
- Members of the Black Asian Minority Ethnic Community (BAME)
- Those with pre-existing health issues e.g. heart conditions, obesity, diabetes

That some of these groups include the more vulnerable indicates how Covid19 has begun to change previous societal norms.

What ethical issues were raised? In relation to Covid19 the key ethical issues, some of which continue, seemed to be:

- Whether it is acceptable to ration the provision of health care and related resources to parts of the population and so exclude others on the basis of age, health status, ethnicity etc?
- Whether it is acceptable to ask the whole of society to relinquish the freedom of associating and decisions on mobility (Lockdown) primarily to benefit particular cohorts in the population? (Stay Home, Save the NHS, Save Lives)
- Whether it is acceptable to ask groups engaged in primary healthcare in hospitals, care homes and the community to work without appropriate protection (PPE) in situations where risks were less than completely quantified?

These basic questions resulted in consequential questions of which the most important were:

- Is it acceptable to disadvantage some groups e.g. children of school age? students in higher and further education? by pausing their learning for an unspecified period so as to potentially protect others, such as those over 70 years of age?
- Is it acceptable to close down the ability to carry out some occupations e.g. restaurants, theatre, retail, horticulture if the consequence is of them being unable ever to re-open and resulting in the permanent loss of many well-paid jobs?
- How legitimate is it for governments to take decisions without being willing to fully share the information on which its decisions are based?
- How justifiable is it for government to communicate messages which may be generally true but wrong in specific instances?

- Is it appropriate to prioritise hope over realism?
- How should the appropriate time for ending Lockdown be established and how might the impact of public boredom be avoided – a bit like children on a long car journey constantly asking, 'Are we nearly there?'

Reflections on the Pandemic

At the time of writing over 41,000 people have died with Covid19 in the UK alone and millions worldwide. Every life lost has been a tragedy for the individual and for their friends and family. As the virus which is the cause of this pandemic is small and essentially invisible, it is easy to assume that all that has occurred has nothing to do with us; to envision it as almost 'an act of God' and perhaps a parallel to the flood discussed in Chapter 10. The origin of this virus, from related viruses which are native in the bat population but tolerated in bats as a consequence of their high metabolic rate, was a natural phenomenon. Such phenomena are well known. Its spread and its impact on humanity were not inevitable. Spread and impact were all a result of the ways in which we have constructed contemporary society e.g. housing inequalities, health inequalities, international travel. This must inevitably require reflection on what we need to learn, not just from what was done rightly or wrongly in how we responded, but what we might do to redesign society so as to minimise the impact of future viruses. Much of this would also have been true of the Black Death in the fourteenth century.

- What allowed a disease which began in one place to become something which had major impact on the whole world?
- What were the key steps which moved an infection from central China to the world as a whole?
- What does the impact of Covid19 say about our certainty of being in control?

Inadvertently the social and commercial structure of the modern world had unforeseen and unintended consequences. As a society were we culpable?

The primary driver of the extent and speed of the spread appeared to be international trade and travel. Individuals infected in one part of the world travelled to other parts taking the viral infection with them.

The second was the extent of social interactions through mass gatherings ranging from shopping to sporting fixtures and church services.

The third may have been inadequate hygiene practices which facilitated the transfer of the virus from commonly touched surfaces and coughing.

The fourth stemmed from an increasing concentration of people into cities, and within those cities, significant concentrations of people living in poorer quality housing. In countries, such as the UK, concentrating people in selected areas of the country, such as Greater London, has been government policy. High density occupation has been a consequence of this, as has an economic policy which has increased mere 'living wage' jobs.

Fifthly a range of issues have facilitated infection. Some link to Climate Change. For example, transport structures have sometimes led, to poor air quality with high concentrations of nitrogen oxides which have impacted on health and increased susceptibility to Covid19. Poor diets, a function of modern living, have led to a rise in obesity, a predisposing factor to serious infections.

Does Scripture help? Covid19 asks questions about 'what it means to be human' questions of sapiential ethics.[56] Why are some individuals more badly impacted than others – issues discussed within Wisdom Literature? Job having given up hope of attaining support and help from his friends makes his plea to God. Job shows both the ultimate of despair:

For now, I shall sleep in the dust and thou shall seek me in the morning but I shall not be.[57]

And hope:

For I know that my redeemer liveth and that he shall stand at the latter day upon the earth.[58]

Wisdom is about priorities, something where Jesus gave clear guidance.[59] Jesus did not to say that we ought not to worry about illnesses but that

---

56 Crenshaw JL (1998) *Old Testament Wisdom*, John Knox Press, Kentucky.

57 Job 7: 21 (KJV).

58 Job 19: 25-26 (KJV).

59 E.g. Luke 17: 33.

getting your life in order and being concerned about what really mattered was key. Fear has been a major feature of the Covid19 outbreak. Fear has generated worry. Perspective and confidence in personal autonomy are important. Jesus said,

Life is more than food, the body more than clothes . . . Can anxious thought add a day to your life?[60]

Coping with fear and the ability to adjust to this fear has been a significant issue and tells us much about the mental vulnerability of humanity. The Wisdom Literature guides us when we venture into an area with the ability to make fundamental changes and to rebuild, something which Job had to do. When the people of Israel were journeying in the wilderness with Moses, he gave them the Ten Commandments [61] which over time were expanded into a large number of rules giving more detailed guidance on more subjects. Jesus made it both simpler but with the need for more reflection when he reduced commandments to the most basic:

Love the Lord your God with all your heart . . . and your neighbour as yourself.[62]

Jesus' approach made life more complicated.[63] His followers were required to think and to work out what was needed. This is true of much about modern life. We are trained to think. We are encouraged to take responsibility for our choices. The move from regimented to individual has been a feature of the current world both at work and in life. Covid19 has reversed much of this. In the UK we had had constant repetition of the mantra 'Stay at home, Protect our NHS and Save lives'. Much of what had become established practice was set aside. Years of actions to stop the loneliness experienced by older citizens was set aside as part of 'Lockdown'. Education and the need for children to be at school for every day of the School year suddenly ceased to be that important. The previous need for thought and analysis was suddenly unnecessary and even undesirable. Our veneer of culture was shown to be rather thin.

---

60 Luke 12: 23, 25.
61 Deuteronomy 5: 6-21.
62 Luke 10: 27, taken from Deuteronomy 6: 5 and Leviticus 19: 18.
63 As in Matthew 5: 17-20.

What will change?

At the beginning of this chapter a number of the initial impacts of Covid19 were reviewed. A consequence of the virus has been elements of life as we knew it being re-addressed. Among these are the following:

Reality Rethink Recalibrate.[64] For months we lived in a world of 3-word mantras from the UK Government – exhorting us to do our bit to beat the virus. When Lockdown eased, we were invited to envisage what lay ahead. The new world could be summed up as – *Reality* demands that we all *Rethink* our priorities and lifestyle and Government will have to *Recalibrate* budgets and manifesto aims.

As winter approaches how will the NHS cope if this virus still prevails? Will the 'trolleys-in-the-corridors' nightmare somehow disappear? Flu and Norovirus may not take a winter off.

There is increasing well documented evidence of the effect on mental health as a result of forced isolation and lack of normal human contact and interaction. Mental health provision for adults and children has been woefully short in supply to date – how then can provision be conjured up to deal with the predicted increased mental health problems arising from Lockdown and the potential PTSD effects of the traumas experienced by medical and caring staff and those who were on ventilators?

Will catch-up be possible in relation to delayed operations and treatment of cancers, hip replacements and other electives. Never before has the old Arabian proverb, 'He that has Health has Hope, He that has Hope has Everything' seemed so relevant – but maybe never so hard to achieve.

Church. How we worship has changed dramatically. It has been necessary to rethink church. The traditional pattern of church going came to an end. It was one of the earliest casualties of the Lockdown. In itself, this is significant. In no other national crisis have churches been closed but this time they were among the first closed and the last opened. They were no longer seen as an integral component in our response to the greatest single challenge of our era. Perhaps the other indicator of a decreasing role for the church was that none in its senior leadership seemed to object. They had moved to thinking in a secular way. Many appeared to

---

64 This section is a Reflection provided by Margaret Hadley.

have become managers rather than pastors or prophets. Worship which has ever been communal was forced to move onto an individual basis. Prayer, the reading of Scripture, confession and reflection continued but as individual rather than shared activities. Central features of the normal pattern of worship, such as the shared Eucharist ended. Religious activity found a new means of expression through the use of the Internet. Worship was streamed from church buildings where only the celebrant was present, Zoom and related means were used to hold events ranging from worship to coffee mornings. The new approach to the public expression of faith appeared to involve greater numbers than were previously present at Sunday Worship. Traditional Church might have ended, but phoenix like, Electronic Church came to life.

Beyond electronic life people rediscovered ways to refresh their spiritual life. As part of the Lockdown Regulations exercise and especially walking was encouraged. Large numbers took advantage of the opportunity to leave the house. Wilder areas such as riversides, open grassland and especially woodland became places for reflection. Unbuilt-on spaces have long had such a role. Satish Kumar[65] emphasised this when asked about attaining consciousness. He emphasised the importance of walking. Walking was a way of touching the earth and providing a window into the mind of God. Going slowly created the space to encounter the sacred. Will pilgrimages of this type, once a key element in church, return as a significant component in being church? Issues related to this have recently been reviewed in the journal of the Scottish Episcopal Institute.[66] Pilgrimages can either be physical or intellectual and so have the potential to develop faith in ways with the flexibility to cope with ever changing rules on life in a Covid19 afflicted world.

In her biography of the writer John Buchan, her grandfather, Ursula Buchan[67] recalled the formative impact of wild areas upon him. He found spending time among the woods, hills and waters allowed solitude, time to appreciate beauty and to contemplate heritage. There will be major changes within our churches. Before the current restriction no-one would have

---

65 Kumar S (2009) 'Is there a simple way to attain consciousness?' pp. 22-23.

66 *Scottish Episcopal Institute Journal*, No 4.3, Autumn 2020.

67 Buchan U (2019) *Beyond the Thirty-Nine steps: A life of John Buchan*, Bloomsbury, London.

believed that churches could have been closed and worship undertaken without meeting. What elements are critical and which merely residual tradition? For some this may lead to digital technologies. For others it will emphasise the centrality of the Eucharist. Perhaps above all it emphasises that the survival of church must be rooted in the notion that the church is not a building.

Employment. The role of employment in life was changed by the advent of the virus both in terms of its centrality to the organisation of society and national economies. Funds were found to pay, for a limited time, many who were not able to be at work. New rules were introduced, on a temporary basis, to prevent those who had lost income and were renting their accommodation from being evicted and so becoming homeless. As I write it remains unclear how these issues will be resolved.

While many roles came under threat of disappearing it became clear that there was an opportunity to make significant changes to the focus of employment. We had become over reliant on importing manufactured goods. Previous approaches to business had adversely impacted the environment. There were new areas which could provide substantial jobs. Coming to terms with Covid19 needed a vaccine. Modern bioscience which is at the heart of this book represents a potential area for business growth. Genome Editing could have a role in meaningful job creation.[68] CRISPR technologies can have a range of impacts. Is there a genetic basis for differential susceptibility to Covid19? The enhanced susceptibility of BAME people suggests so. Should we be using genome therapies and embryonic Genome Editing methods to make individuals resistant? The first Genome Edited humans were edited for resistance to a virus.

Risk. How we view risk has become an important element in our response to Covid19. Would doing this put ourselves at risk, would it endanger others, have become important questions? This was the core of the UK Government's daily messaging. What has become clear is that we need a more sophisticated understanding of risk. The word 'risk' lacks a clear and universal meaning. Terms such as 'at risk' seem meaningless. Ought people of faith have a different attitude to risk? Where is God within our approach to risk? Most activities involve trade-offs in relation to the benefits of the activity and risk. Risk involves elements of both the

---

68 Carey N (2020).

probability of it happening and the consequences if it does. If we perceive the risk to be low, we are likely to chance it unless the consequences, should the worst happen are severe. Judging risk is an important element in independent life. Human survival depends upon an ability to study the complexity of life and then to cope with reality as it presents itself in the circumstances of normal existence. This is an ability it matters that we re-acquire.

Haven't We Been Here Before?

In Chapter 1 past pandemics such as the Black Death were compared to Covid19. It might be argued that something which happened in the fourteenth century when the world was very different can be of no relevance to the different situation that we find today. Alternatively, the time that has passed has given time for the full impact to be seen. For those who survived the Black Death material prospects were good but could not compensate for the impact of the suffering which it was assumed had a sapiential cause and was the will of God. The impact of the Plague was substantial and so can inform reflections on our future beyond Covid19. Some consequences were to be expected, other unexpected. What were the Black Death's residual effects?

- A religious revival but increased questioning of how to form a relationship with God.
- Changed moral standards.
- Parliamentary government, the House of Commons and the role of Speaker came into being around 1343 because of the Crown's need to raise taxes.
- Food production and agriculture were reformed.
- A search for scapegoats. Jewish people were blamed.

Despite the severity of the plague other things continued to happen. 1346 saw the Battle of Crecy, a part of the continuing war between England and France.

Life has a strange way of repeating itself.

Chapter 4

Two Science Journeys

Two major strands emerge from the Science which introduced this book (Chapter2) and which make up the Science story with which the book closes (Chapter12) – Health and Food. Together these remain among the most important elements of life as we know it. They also represent two of the most important markets for technologies such as CRISPR Genome Editing. As well as Science-led issues, wider food and health considerations question how such technologies might be used by society and what societal pressures decide what moves into day-to-day practice and what becomes just a footnote detailing a road not significantly travelled. The new technology raises fundamental questions which are common to both and will attract a similar critical examination. It seemed appropriate to review these commonalities in a joint chapter before moving to the detail of individual potential uses. The context to all that follows in this chapter is, how might we best make use of Genome Editing? These questions seemed important for people of faith. In 2017 the Scottish Episcopal Church's Church and Society Committee set up a working group on Genome Editing under the chairmanship of Donald Bruce. Significant amounts of the material in Chapters 5 and 6 are a product of discussions held by that group of which I was a member.

The Science Journey: Health[69]

Health care from where it began to the present has been a journey which has involved both technical issues and societal responses. The introduction to Science practice and the subsequent use of Embryonic Stem Cells (1997) raised important questions about both when life begins

---

69 The scientific basis of issues covered here are detailed in Chapter 12, in the sections on Viruses, HeLa Cells, Polio, Organ Transplantation, Epigenetics, IVF, Stem Cells, the Human Genome and Genome Editing.

and the relative value of individuals and societal groups.[70] Embryonic stem cells are capable of giving rise to any type of cell. Initially they were needed to produce cells used to repair damaged or deficient organs especially where that organ did not produce its own stem cells. A range of cells (Pluripotent stem cells) can now be deprogrammed and allowed to become stem cells again. They rarely however have the total flexibility (Totipotent stem cells) of embryonic cells. Embryonic stem cells had to be derived from embryos. This meant the destruction of an embryo. To some the status of the embryo was such that this was not acceptable. This identifies the importance of particular world views which depend on a particular philosophy. In considering issues such as this it is important to note both that such views exist and also that their existence may not always be explicitly recognised. Many decisions contain elements which at their heart question what sacrifice might be needed by which individual or small group so as to benefit a larger group.

Genome Editing also involves and may challenge a number of philosophical positions. It is a new technology with great potential for which many claims have been made. Initial responses to medical uses of Genome Editing have been favourable. However, the acceptability of the approach was questioned in late 2018 when a scientist in China announced that he had used the technology to modify human embryos which were brought to term, resulting in the birth of twin girls with modified genetics (Chapter 5&8). The potential for making changes in the genomes of those who were yet to be born suddenly made discussion a matter of urgency.

As part of the response to Covid19 the question has been asked why some are badly, all too commonly fatally, impacted by the virus while others are only slightly affected. Questions are being asked as to whether this difference has a genetic basis. If this is the case it seems likely that somewhere someone will want to gene-edit embryos so that they are resistant to Covid19. All of this makes it important to address the inherent question at the heart of this volume 'what does it mean to be human?' There continues to be progress in understanding human genetics and its relationship to human disease. Science has always been a driver. There is normally a clear route from the Science to practical application. Clear and tested routes of commercialisation have evolved. Science has driven

---

70 Jones D A (2004) *The Soul of the Embryo*, Continuum, London.

a business model. This model usually involved major international companies leading to major financial and societal support. The new Science of Genome Editing has followed a well-trodden pathway. To date society has been content and supportive of proceeding in this way. The development of such an approach can continue independently of what will certainly be an on-going debate about the modification of embryos. Technologies, such as CRISPR, have a range of potential uses. There would seem to be merit in focusing on potential contributions rather than being over-distracted by broader issues as happened with the introduction of GM crops which are discussed in the next section.

A number of diseases have their basis in a relatively simple mutation of a single gene. Many more, even of those with a clear basis in genetics, are more complex and involve many genes. An approach, which is aimed at extending life, must also cause us to think about how we contemplate disability and death. Assisted dying (discussed in detail in Chapter 9) has long been a matter for debate. Faith organisations and professional bodies have asked if it ought to be legal to assist someone in ending their life. Potential new treatments, such as CRISPR, have been cited as an argument against permitting such a change. The main thrust of discussion relates to questions around the value of life and the costs of preserving life. The question what is a life worth has exercised actuaries and insurers. Are all lives equally of value has long been an unspoken question in society? The Covid19 pandemic has re-raised these questions especially where insufficient resources preclude them being available to all.

Much of the focus of molecular medicine has been centred on understanding the out-working of the genetic code. Not all genes are expressed in all situations. This is critical to cell differentiation. Every cell in a body has the same genome but it matters that heart cells should develop in one way and that skin or liver cells should develop differently. For this to occur some genes will need to be activated (up-regulated) and others will need to be silenced (down-regulated). This switching process depends upon where a stem cell finds itself. This has been used to de-programme cells and return them to a near embryonic state for use in gene therapy.

Environment can influence the effective genome i.e. the individual genes that are or are not activated. Understanding this switching on and off process is the basis of epigenetics. Problems in the programming of cell types lead to cells misbehaving which can result in cancers. Science currently offers two distinct but related approaches. Genome Editing can be used in correcting mutations and to restoring what might be regarded as a healthy gene. Alternatively, epigenetics provides a means of changing the functioning of existing genes, and as a result cell programming. That the functioning, the expression, of the genome can be modified by its environment (Chapter 12) has wide implications. Epigenetic changes may also open a new approach to understanding issues in relation to sexuality and to gender expression. This raises new challenges for traditional faith-based understanding and approaches.

The Science Journey: Food[71]

Most of the societal issues in relation to health have their parallels in food production. This is especially true for animal-based products and the use of livestock. Behind most apparently superficial technical differences in approach to agriculture are significantly different approaches to incorporating key values. The development of agriculture in the second half of the last century illustrates this in a helpful way. The period between 1960 and 1990 saw the introduction of the chemical control of pests, weeds and diseases as the most common approach to crop protection in 'developed countries' and resulted in such a form of farming being described as 'conventional production'. Over the same period Organic Farming developed and was codified. How these two approaches differ, and their advantages and disadvantages, should simply be a discussion of practical alternatives to resource use within food production. The difference in approach has however become an increasingly bitter division. The difference represents a proxy battle over core values within society. Dangerously, to this battle are linked the profitability of significant international industrial companies.

Chemical crop protection sees unwanted plants, insects and fungi as an enemy which need to be eradicated This is a war to be won. Many crop protection chemicals have names, such as 'Stomp', which reflect this war-like attitude. In contrast organic production recognises that unwanted organisms are restraints to production but has developed an approach based on management of risk and on co-existence. There are differences

---

71 The science which underpins this area is detailed in Chapter 12, in the sections on DNA, GM Crops, Cloning, Genome Editing and CRISPR.

in priorities and in the objectives of the enterprises. Supporters of conventional production point to yields, the amount of food which can potentially be produced and to the proportion of the world's population which *might* be fed. Supporters of organic production point to beneficial impacts on the environment, the contribution to global employment and the greater involvement of people in food production. It is important to remember that higher yields do not always result in greater amounts reaching to consumer.

Food is a wide and diverse concept. The Scottish Government's 2009 Food Strategy[72] went beyond mere food production. The policy encompassed issues linked to: Who has access to food? Of what quality? Is food affordable? How does food impact health? Are production and supply chains sustainable? and What risks are there within the system? It considered environmental impact and the Climate Change footprint of the systems. Where the boundaries of a system are set will have a significant impact on what seems the best approach. This has parallels in the discussion of Covid19 and of the potential for elimination compared to a managed co-existence as a possible approach by Government.

The above clash over basic values had a significant role in the debate over the suggested introduction of GM (Genetically Modified) food 25 years ago. An awareness of an increasing global population was headlined as the driver of the need for the production of GM crops. An increased global population, it was argued, would need increased food production. There would be a reduction in the quantity of agricultural land per capita as global population increased. The only solution was producing more food per unit area of land, i.e. the intensification of production. To meet this end, it was argued, the World needed to embrace developed world solutions which included GM crops. Traditional approaches such as organic production it was claimed would not be able to deliver the needed yields and should be abandoned. Such arguments ignore the impact of wastage which is increased by the complex food chains commonly involved with conventional developed world agriculture and the significant variation in production between different countries and years.

---

72 Scottish Government (2009) *Recipe for Success – Scotland's National Food and Drink Policy.*

The yields of our major crops, such as wheat, maize, soya, had all been increasing for much of the twentieth century as plant breeding improved. Improvements were based on both the contribution of individual genes, which became better understood, and on the ways in which gene exchanges between species/cultivars had become more effective. Despite an increase in the precision of traditional breeding/crossing methods there was inevitably much hit and miss involved in the process. For example, it could take some years to remove the unwanted genes co-transferred with desirable genes during the crossing process.

Genetic modification was highlighted as a major advance and the way to speed up the crop breeding process. With this technology only the desired genes were transferred. There were no undesirable co-transferees to remove. The ability to insert new genes into crop plants would allow the production of crops which had been precisely modified though the introduction of genes, most commonly from bacteria, to give crops radical new properties. While industry stressed precision and the ability to make precise changes, closer examination showed that this was not always so. Novel genes were commonly introduced by a shot-gun approach, where minute gold pellets coated with the novel DNA were fired into a tissue culture resulting in some cells receiving the novel gene but with limited control over the position of insertion.

In addition, most of the early GM varieties had modifications linked to production rather than to quality traits. The first GM Crops were modified to be resistant to herbicides or insect pests. The manufacturers of agrochemicals seemed to be the principal beneficiaries. Any risks however were carried by society. As a result, the public in much of Europe were unconvinced of the need for such crops or the safety of the approach. Fundamentally they did not see what was in it for them. This approach seemed to facilitate a direction of travel which was already a matter of concern, a further intensification of agricultural production. Following on from the publication of Rachel Carson's classic book 'Silent Spring'[73] there was unease as to whether this was the desired way to go. The major issues that came through the debates were expressed in a rather different way. Many thought that such approaches were simply 'unnatural'. The population in general was unconvinced that GM was either the only solution or even

---

73 Carson R (1963) *Silent Spring*, Hamish Hamilton, London.

the best solution to the needs of a rising global population. For the public as a whole, food and food production were seen as more than just an issue about yields.

Food has a wide societal context which is probably why it is among the most frequently referenced subjects in the Hebrew Scriptures (Chapter2). They contain many rules/laws related to food production. Worldwide food production is responsible for social structures of many developing countries. In his 1976 Bawden Lecture to the British Crop Protection Council's Annual Conference, a meeting dominated by International Crop Protection Industries, the American Scientist Leroy Holme[74] argued that the introduction of agro-chemicals into agriculture across the world, and especially into the developing world, would end back-breaking manual cultivation and release people to follow other less strenuous occupations. This ignored the embedding of food production within so many cultures. Changes in approaches to food production in the developing world have however occurred over recent years. Small farmers have moved from rural communities but all too often to poorly paid employment or no employment in cities.

The claims made in the 1990s for the potential role of GM crops in global food production were seen by many to be a repeat of an earlier chemical vision about which there was considerable scepticism. Many seemed clear that agriculture was just more complex than whether a particular crop produced ten tonnes per hectare or only nine. The role of GM foods in the diet remains an issue and a significant element in international trade talks. All of this sets the stage for a coming debate as to whether Genome Editing can be generally acceptable in a way that GM crops were not. Genome Editing has significant differences to the GM approach. It is more precise. It seems likely to have a different pattern of introduction. The relatively imprecise result of insertion using GM technologies resulted in their first being used with crop plants. The precision of Genome Editing makes it likely that initial developments may happen in farm animals. The smaller genomes found in animals – all vertebrate animals are diploids having just two sets of chromosomes – make it easier for Genome Editing to have an effect. The larger genome of many crop plants (strawberries are octoploids

---

74 Holme L (1998) 'The importance of weeds in world food production', pp. 31-46 in the Bawden Memorial Lecture, ed. T Lewis BCPC, Farnham, Surrey.

with eight sets of chromosomes) make it much harder for Genome Editing to have significant effects.

Conclusion

What is clear in relation to the use of new biological technologies in both health and food is that they have the potential to impact life as we know it. They raise issues about subjects which are discussed in Scripture. They question the selection of ways in which society may wish to develop, and also its understanding of core values. The range of issues is covered in detail in the chapters which follow.

Chapter 5

Biotechnology and Health[75]

Molecular Biology has now been around in its current form for over 30 years.[76] The advent of CRISPR less than a decade ago has now made, things of Science Fiction real practical possibilities.[77] It questions how we make use of this new knowledge.[78] Humans are animals. This is a biological fact. Gene editing works in animals, such as mice, so there is every reason to think that it ought to work in humans. There are well tried approaches for moving things from animals to humans but there is always the risk of someone somewhere just trying the technology, perhaps on themselves. The entry costs of the CRISPR technology are relatively low. This is a real risk. Society needs to reflect on the role of these technologies. There are particular questions for people of faith.

Beginning the story

Why should society at large be interested in Genome Editing? We are aware that many human lives are cut short or severely restricted by genetically based 'diseases'. CRISPR holds out the very real prospect of repairing faults in the genetic code of sufferers. Many new developments in Science begin by offering something of value but then develop in ways that were not foreseen. Given its importance are there limits to the ways in which we would want to see Genome Editing used? Are there limits to the disorders that should be treated? We may be content with its use on adults, but would it be acceptable to modify a human embryo with the certainty

---

75 Underlying science relevant to this chapter is covered in Chapter 12 in the sections on DNA, RNA, IVF, Stem cells, the Human Genome, Genome Editing and CRISPR.

76 Marshall G and Atkinson D (1991) *Molecular Biology: Its practice and role in crop protection*, BCPC, Farnham, Surrey.

77 Doudna J and Sternberg SH (2017) *A Crack in Creation*, Bodley Head, London.

78 Carey N (2020) *Hacking the Code of Life: How Gene Editing Will Rewrite our Futures*, Icon Books, London.

that this would impact future generations? This is a multi-layered question as there are already concerns about any use of embryos in research.[79]

So, what exactly is Genome Editing? The genetic code of humans and an increasing number of organisms have been mapped. The sequence of bases, which make up the genetic code, the DNA code found in most organisms (all eukaryotes), has been determined. The DNA code is responsible for the nature of the proteins we produce. Structural proteins make up our bodies. Hormones, enzymes, and growth factors influence so much of our development and day-to-day maintenance. There is now good understanding of what many of our genes do and the ways in which they effect that control.

The most frequently referenced Genome Editing system is CRISPR/ Cas9. CRISPR is the abbreviation for *Clustered Regularly Interspaced Short Palindromic Repeats*. You can see why it needs the abbreviation. It is found in bacteria and it's one of the mechanisms which they use to resist attacks by viruses. CRISPR identifies a sequence of DNA. Cas9 is the enzymic 'scissors' and makes the cuts. Once the DNA has been cut it is then possible to add additional base-pair material to effect either change or additions. Genome Editing can thus be used to cut the DNA code at a chosen location so as to repair mistakes in the letters, which make up the code, either to change the ways in which genes are expressed or to insert new material and so change the genes to something that was not there before, as a repair or extension.

We can think of such techniques as being like a pair of scissors, which can be used to cut out damaged areas in a piece of material. This creates the options of either sewing up the hole or allowing the insertion of a patch to fill the hole. The new material can either be identical to the original or different to what was there before. In terms of the concept and its molecular biology it really is as simple as that.

Case Studies

A girl dying from leukaemia. Layla Richards was a one year old child dying of an aggressive leukaemia which was affecting her bone marrow and immune system. Layla had been diagnosed with acute lymphoblastic leukaemia at three months of age, at Great Ormond Street Children's Hospital

---

79 Jones DA (2004) *The Soul of the Embryo*, Continuum, London.

in London. All conventional treatments had failed. She was saved by the use of engineered immune cells from a donor. As a last-ditch attempt to save her life she was given a transfusion of immune cells (T-cells) which had been modified by Genome Editing to withstand rejection. Within a month the T-cells had killed the cancerous cells in Layla's bone marrow, and after three months she was given a second bone marrow transplant to restore her immune system. She made what seems to have been a complete recovery.

This rare example is heart-warming. New technology saved a life. It is highly unorthodox because it used a novel approach to immune therapy which had previously only been tried in mice. This was a 'medical exception' – where a person, who is so seriously ill that death is inevitable and imminent, is given an unproven treatment that might be able to save their life. The Layla Richards case raises questions. Should such exceptions be granted for children with less serious disorders? It is important to distinguish between the ethics of emergency and normal situations. Even after this single success, detailed clinical trials to establish how widely and safely such a novel method could be applied would be necessary. Individual cases could be decided only on clinical evidence. This may not yet be clear enough to prescribe a treatment safely.

The CRISPR bombshell. At a conference on Human Genome Editing held in November 2018 in Hong Kong, a Chinese Scientist, Professor So He Jiankui, reported the birth of two genome edited twin baby girls, Lulu and Nana. He had used CRISPR technology and In Vitro Fertilisation (IVF) to modify human embryos at a very early developmental stage, following which they were implanted in their mother's uterus. The babies had been modified to be resistant to HIV. At the time the scientific community had concluded such an approach would not be responsible given the current state of knowledge. The technology had previously been used on human embryos but not on ones brought to term. Again, there are questions about when life begins.[80] Lulu and Nana may be the first to pass intentional mutations to their children. The editing involved the transfer of a mutant CCR5 Gene. The un-mutated gene makes a protein allowing HIV to infect cells. Some people naturally have the mutated form of the gene which confers resistance. The stated aim of the exercise was to protect the children from contracting HIV, a viral disease. The existing gene was changed using

---

80 Jones DA (2004).

CRISPR to produce the variant. However, it is possible that these children will be more susceptible to influenza. Initial tests on the children suggested that there were no off-target mutations. That this transformation was to give resistance to a virus has added significance in the post Covid19 era.

Elijah. Elijah was one of the earliest of the prophets. He is most commonly remembered for his disputes with the Prophets of Baal[81] and his conversations with God.[82] He is also remembered for a healing miracle, which links to Layla Richards.

> *The son of the woman, (the widow of Zarephath) fell ill and was in a very bad way until at last his breathing stopped. The woman said to Elijah, 'What made you interfere you man of God? You came here to bring my sins to light, and cause my son's death!' 'Give me your son,' he said. He took the boy from her arms and carried him up to the roof chamber and laid him on his bed. He called out to the Lord, 'Lord my God, is this your care for the widow with whom I lodge that you have been so cruel to her son?' Then he breathed deeply on the child three times and called to the Lord, 'I pray Lord my God, let the breath of life return to the body of this child.' The Lord listened to Elijah's cry and the breath of life returned to the child's body and he revived. Elijah lifted him and took him down from the roof chamber into the house, and giving him to his mother he said, 'Look, your son is alive.' She said to Elijah, 'Now I know for certain that you are a man of God and that the word of the Lord on your lips is truth.'*
> (1 Kings 17: 17-24)

Elijah causes us to reflect on healing, miraculous healing events and the role of God in all that happens. Do miracles still happen? In the Introduction to this book I suggest the importance of reconsidering just what we would regard as a miracle in today's world? Do all miracles have to be supernatural? How differently are things regarded in society in general and by people of faith.? How might we connect Elijah and CRISPR? Was Layla Richards' healing a miracle? If such treatments were to become more common would that make them less miraculous? Were the births of Lulu and Nana a miracle? We are at a stage where it matters to consider such questions. These are real issues for discussion to which we return later.

---

81 1 Kings 18: 25-40.
82 E.g. 1 Kings 19: 9-18.

Health and Ethical Issues

CRISPR/Cas9 allows us to edit the genetic code and repair mistakes in the 'letters'. Changes to a single letter are possible. In humans, gene editing can be used to repair damaged DNA, which could enable treatments for devastating genetic diseases, in both adults and children (*Somatic Gene Therapy*). The most controversial applications relate to the possibility of altering the genes of an early human embryo (*Germline Therapy*). This can be used as part of basic research into the development of the embryo, and where there is no intention to implant the embryo, or, as in the Chinese experiments, where genes were edited in human embryos then implanted in the womb, and born as genetically altered babies.

Somatic Gene Therapy. Many human diseases and conditions are caused by defects in one or more genes. This includes illnesses such as Cystic Fibrosis, Huntington's Disease, Hyperargininaemia, Immunodeficiency, Muscular Dystrophy, Sickle Cell Anaemia, Whim Syndrome, and some Cancers. For some years gene therapy has attempted to correct some of these conditions in adults and children, with limited success. It is now possible, using genome editors, to correct or replace a defective gene with a normal one at its natural location. The aim is that corrected genes will either preferentially re-populate the tissues, or be present in sufficient quantities and for long enough to bring the 'disease' under control. Most commonly cells are taken from a patient who is suffering from a 'disease' caused by a single genetic defect. Genome Editing is used to correct the defect and the cells are then returned to the patient. A future example might be someone suffering from Type 1 Diabetes which is the result of faults in the production of insulin from the pancreas. If it were possible to remove cells from the patient, genome edit them to correct the genetic fault and replace the cells which were now able to produce insulin, this would represent an important new approach to therapy. Using the patient's own cells would avoid rejection.

It is thus possible to use CRISPR/Cas9 to modify the functioning of an organ within a patient. These genetic changes are specific to the individual and are not passed on to any subsequent offspring. As such it is generally considered ethically acceptable, subject to the normal safety and ethical requirements which apply to any novel therapy. There are currently over twenty clinical trials underway worldwide to test somatic gene therapy using Genome Editing. How will this be developed? We can question the impact of funding being provided from commercial or from government sources. This seems likely to influence the priorities for development.[83] If significant numbers are to benefit from the technology it needs to be applied to a disease which impacts many and where the possibility of success is high. Illnesses where there are a variety of genetic forms would not be a good choice. Success will require knowledge of how the illness is caused. The genetics needs to be sufficiently understood so that the genetic changes to be made are clear. This rules out diseases caused by more than one gene and those where there is significant interaction between the working of the gene and its environment. Key questions include: How certain are you that the change will have the effect intended? Can the edit be got to the right tissue? Will it survive long enough to have an effect? Will the changes be able to be transferred to daughter cells?

As a result, many of the most common and debilitating illness will not be early candidates for treatment. However, there are diseases which are potentially treatable and could beneficially impact significant numbers – Sickle Cell Anaemia is an example. This disease results from problems with the protein haemoglobin which is found in red blood cells. Haemoglobin binds to oxygen and supplies it to cells within the body via the blood stream. Haemoglobin is made of 4 protein chains, two alpha chains and two beta chains. Sickle Cell disease is a genetic disorder which causes a defect in the beta chain of haemoglobin. This causes problems in the uptake and transfer of oxygen. Sickle Cell Anaemia affects many people in the developing world, can be easily diagnosed and the genetic change required is clear. A mutant gene exists within the human population which results in adults retaining a form of haemoglobin which is more usual in a foetus. The current approach to dealing with the Sickle Cell Disease is to take bone marrow from patients with a haemoglobin disorder, edit the DNA in the lab so that the changed cells have the protective mutation. These are used as stem cells and reinjected into bone marrow. This has allowed the production of a standard gene editing protocol which ought to work on all patients. A single copy of the mutant gene seems to confer some resistance to Malaria.

---

83 Carey N (2020) *Hacking the Code of Life: How Gene Editing Will Rewrite our Futures*, Icon Books, London.

Human Genome Editing for embryo research. Issues related to the use of human embryos for any purpose other than to produce a living child have always been contentious.[84] It is clear that the beginning of each human life, and thus the fate and status of the embryo, is a matter of wide concern and one which goes beyond the limits of biology or medicine. It is a technical, ethical, societal and theological problem simultaneously. Understanding how and when each of us begins is important to thoughts about the treatment of the embryo outside of the womb. The use of IVF in humans allowed the birth of the first 'test tube' baby in 1978. However standard IVF techniques result in the production of more embryos than are normally transferred in a single treatment cycle. This has led to the production of thousands of 'spare embryos'. These have been seen as a resource for Science and a succession of UK laws have allowed an increasing scope for the types of research which is permitted.

In 2017 the UK Human Fertilisation and Embryology Authority (HFEA) made a landmark decision to grant a licence for research at the Francis Crick Institute involving Genome Editing of human embryos. Researchers inactivated the OCT4 gene and found that the cells, which would eventually form the placenta, developed more, but that the embryo failed to form its next (blastocyst) stage. This was quite different from what had been seen in mouse studies. This illustrated both the importance of this gene and the limitations of mouse models in an understanding of human biology. The HFE Act expressly forbids any genetically modified embryo being implanted. Embryos used in research are destroyed at day 7. This destruction of an embryo which had the potential to become a person is at the heart of the objections to this type of study.

Ethical issues and embryo research. Research using human embryos raises significant ethical issues. Society and Christians are honestly divided. Some believe that from the point of fertilisation the human embryo should be considered to have the same moral status as a new-born baby. Thus, to perform research and then destroy the embryo should be absolutely forbidden. Even research for the benefit of other embryos would be considered to violate the absolute value of the sacrificed embryo. These objections were at the heart of resistance to the development of embryonic stem cell cultures.

---

84 Jones DA (2004).

Others think that moral status develops with time, and would accept limited research up to the current UK legal limit of 14 days from fertilisation. This view was articulated by the then Bishop of Oxford in the House of Lords in 2000. *Developing reality is associated with developing rights.*[85] This would lead to the embryo having a special but not an absolute status. By around 14 days, implantation in the womb is normally complete, establishing a physical relationship with the mother; the embryo's individuality is confirmed and after this the primitive central nervous system begins to form. Another important factor for some in respect of the status of the embryo, is that the majority of fertilisations spontaneously abort anyway within these early days of development. In humans not all embryos lead to the birth of a child.

Some couples, having gone through IVF programmes which result in 'surplus' embryos, donate these embryos and give consent for them to be used in research. The notion of this being a gift is deeply important. Is there a danger that embryo research may become 'normalised'? Might the common perception move from seeing each human embryo as a potential human being, and thus as a precious gift, to its being viewed as a laboratory consumable? Should human embryo research happen only where there is no alternative and a substantial likelihood of success?

The challenges to being human? A group set up by the Scottish Episcopal Church's Church in Society Committee[86] asked: What does it mean to be human when faced with such far-reaching developments? They identified a framework of assumptions and questions to aid discussion of the issues. The following summarises some of the questions they raised.

First, there is an obvious ethical attraction to eliminating serious and incurable genetic disease by correcting an underlying genetic defect in the embryo, so that the child and his/her subsequent offspring do not develop a disease that had devastated previous generations. In doing this are the new child's genetics simply being restored to how they ought to have been? This of course asks how we understand disability.

Second are we entitled to change the genetic makeup of future individuals?

---

85 Harries R (1995) *Questioning Belief,* SPCK, London.
86 Genome Editing Working Group of SEC (2019) 'What it means to be human', report presented to the 2019 Meeting of General Synod of the SEC.

Third, there are questions about risk. Genetic damage to other parts of the genome by the method of insertion was a problem in the GM era. Is it being sufficiently reduced by the specificity of CRISPR?[87] The gene being edited may have multiple functions so will any changes have unintended consequences?[88] Are there deleterious side effects likely to emerge over subsequent generations? It seems clear that assessing risks without multigenerational human trials, which would be ethically unacceptable, would be impossible. Will it be possible to differentiate such risks from natural genetic mutations?

Fourth, are there diseases so severe, that such risks might be contemplated? What about Huntington's Disease? This is an incurable degenerative condition with extremely distressing mental and physical effects. Its onset is in middle life which can mean the disease may already have been passed on to any existing offspring of that person. It is caused by a single dominant genetic mutation. In principle it could be repaired by the use of CRISPR in the embryo. Whatever risks there might be, would they be few enough?

Fifth, are there serious alternatives? Pre-implantation Genetic Diagnosis (PGD) is currently used with families known to carry a genetic disease. IVF is used to produce an embryo which is screened by removing one cell at the 8-cell stage. Only embryos without the genetic defect are implanted. This would stop the condition being passed on and *without* germ-line therapy. Embryos carrying the disease gene are likely to be produced then destroyed. Could PGD render germ-line therapy unnecessary?

Sixth, will Genome Editing impact the availability of existing treatments for others? The question of priority of course became a real issue during the Covid19 outbreak. Novel therapies compete for resources. If Genome Editing is a success long-term health care may be avoided, but perhaps at the expense of more basic care. How might we strike the correct balance?

Seventh, the history of Science is replete with instances of the raising of unrealistic and ultimately unfilled expectations. Is this a significant concern with Genome Editing?

---

87 Atkinson D (1998) 'Lighting up the soil', pp. 30-32 in *Engineering Genesis,* ed. D Bruce and A Bruce, Earthscan, London.
88 Carey N (2020).

These ethical questions matter profoundly to each of us as individuals and to the future society facing these challenges.

Conclusions

Healing is a major subject in the New Testament and significant in the Hebrew Scriptures. Together they illustrate that issues related to health go beyond mere healing. For example, disability is a complex issue. Disability and suffering have always been a part of the human condition. Christ's compassion provides a model for the healing and caring professions, and motivates a special regard for the those who are different. Will CRISPR impact on how we as a society regard those with disabilities? Will we still be content to pick up the additional costs of the disabled in society? There is evidence that in an era when PGD is on offer, that disabled children, born with a defect that either was or could have been detected, they and their parents are being viewed less sympathetically. What is a disability anyway? All disabilities result in limitations. Most of these can be worked around but some are restrictive to either the length of life or to the quality of life. While disabilities impact on physical activities they also impact on personhood and on who we identify as being like us and on how we see the world. Genome Editing forces us to reflect upon these issues.

What if limitations were not about feasibility but affordability? This is not a new question. Half a century ago questions around family,[89] the right to reproduce,[90] new life forms,[91] the nature of aging[92] and when people ought to be kept alive: these questions were being asked.[93] The issues remain important. Questions, about the status of the embryo, just keep coming up.[94] The longest standing is probably 'Should an embryo be regarded as a person and afforded the protection of that status?' Definitions

89 McLaren A (1972) 'The Future of the Family', pp. 65-76 in *The Future of Man*, ed. FJ Ebling and GW Heath, Academic Press, London.

90 Thoday JM (1972) 'The Right to Reproduce', pp. 77-95, *ibid.*

91 Danielli JF (1972) 'The Artificial Synthesis of New Life Forms in Relation to Social and Industrial Evolution', pp. 95-104, *ibid.*

92 Bellamy D (1972) 'The Nature and Control of Ageing', pp. 113-126, *ibid.*

93 Miller H (1972) 'Keeping People Alive', pp. 127-134, *ibid.*

94 Junker-Kenny M (2002) 'The moral status of the Embryo', pp. 68-75 in *Theological Issues in Bioethics*, ed. N Messer, Darton Longman Todd, London.

have practical implications. Any definition will allow or restrict our ability to act. If life begins at the start of neural activity then prior to that point rules which apply from that point, do not apply and we are free to use the embryo without restriction. Definitions always have practical intent. Maximum protection is given by minimal definition and vice versa. Once commercial interests become involved then any definition will come under pressure to allow development. This is important as we debate the appropriate regulation for the use of CRISPR technologies in relation to embryos.

Does Scripture help? Elijah brought back to life a child who had died. The story involves several elements a caring mother, the child, Elijah's actions, prayer and the power of God. This combination has long been a significant part of the basis of healing. Does modern medicine and genome-editing render this redundant? Does God continue to be involved but in a different way? In cases like that of Layla Richards it seems likely that there was prayer during surgical procedures. Certainly, the coincidence of research on engineered T cells in a University close to where Layla was dying, scientists and doctors in conversation, and a medical exception make for something close to a miracle. Does Genome Editing need us to revisit the question 'where is God in such events?'

If you were asked to list five things that come to mind at the mention of Jesus, healing would be prominent in the list. Many of the healing events associated with Jesus are classed as miracles. The word is used to describe something unexpected and good. Much of popular thinking remains at an elementary level. Miracles are something we accept rather than question. Questioning take us out of our comfort zone. In Matthew's account of the beginning of Jesus' human ministry he tells us about the range of conditions he healed. Healing was commonly linked with what might now be identified as mental issues. Many separate healing events dealt with different ailments such as leprosy, acute pain, fever and paralysis. All we are told is that they all were cured. Peter's mother-in-law was able to minister to Jesus' needs following her cure. A leper was able to resume normal life. A Roman centurion's servant was relieved of his suffering. A paralysed man was able to stand and go home. Whether the healing was permanent we do not know. What it emphasises is the complexity of the healing process. People other than the affected person were involved. Jesus had a reputation for healing. People came to him for healing. Were his later healings which might have been just what was expected from Jesus' lesser miracles because he had done such things before. Can only the 'supernatural' be regarded as miraculous? Scripture tells us of an increasingly close relationship between God and humanity something which has continued over the period after the canon of Scripture was closed. Would it increase the relevance of faith in today's society were we to regard the acts of Science as part of an understanding of a miracle?

What the role of these factors will be in relation to Genome Editing is not clear but past history suggests that there will be issues beyond simple molecular therapy. In a discussion with Nicodemus, Jesus indicated the need to be born again.[95] Nicodemus asked the question:

But how can someone be born again when he is old? Can he enter his mother's womb a second time and be born?

For those with treatable genetic disorders Genome Editing may offer an opportunity to move into a changed life which in some circumstances may be close to being born again, as it was for Layla Richards. Unequivocally Health and Healing are issues where the church is clear that it has a significant remit. Faith that something could be done was a common element in the healings of Jesus.[96]

---

95 John 3: 1-8.
96 E.g. Matthew 8: 2-4, 5-10 and 9: 2-8.

Chapter 6

Biotechnology and Food[97]

In many regards the ways in which we treat and think about the living things – microbes, plants and animals – who are our co-inhabitants of our planet, underpins our attitudes to life. Issues linked to the priority we accord other species tells us much about whether we see ourselves as an integral part of creation or as something which is separate, and for which the rest of creation is a resource (Chapter2). Humanity's use of plants and animals for food has long involved attempts to modify their genetics so as to make them more attuned to human needs. Crop plants, flowering and ornamental species, have been bred for greater yields of the grain, fruit or flowers. Crop breeding relates to the issues of Climate Change (Chapter 10). Animal breeding impacts on living things with whom we share much of our genome and so re-visits many of the issues of Chapter 5.

Beginning the Story

Food production is a key issue. In 1800 the world population was 1billion and in 1987 it reached 5 billion. By the end of this century it may well be 8 billion. This is a result of more people being born but even more a consequence of people living longer. An increasing human population leads to an increase in the quantity of food needed to feed them. While it would be possible to feed an 8 billion population with current food production, it would not be possible to feed such a population on the current western diet. In addition, the current western production system generates significant levels of waste throughout the food chain. However, there is a developing world-wide pressure to increase the consumption of a western diet. Humans are naturally designed to be omnivores and so are best able to survive on a mixed diet, which for much of our history has involved both plant and animal-based components. We recognise that

---

97 The science underpinning developments discussed here is presented in Chapter 12 in the sections on DNA, GM Crops, Cloning, CRISPR.

it is possible to survive on a purely plant-based diet but also that most of the world does not. Hence there is a demand to increase the quantity of both crop and animal-based products[98]. So, what are the limitations? The area of land which is capable of growing crops is limited and while it may be possible to increase this area by the removal of tropical forest, as is currently being done in South America, this has serious implications for Climate Change. If the area of land able to support food production is unable to be expanded, then can we produce more from the same area? This has long been an aspiration and the preceding half century has seen remarkable increases in the crop yields per unit area. A general increase in yields conceals significant variation between countries and years.

Increases have been a product of both the ways in which crops are grown, especially through chemical crop protection, and improved crop genetics. Yield increases have not however been restricted to 'conventional' crop production systems. Yields achieved using approaches such as 'organic' have also increased. Plant breeding has had a major role in increasing food production of all types. Attempts to introduce desirable new traits is always associated with the time needed to remove undesirable traits co-transferred with the desired character during the crossing process. It was to overcome this limitation that genetic modification (GM), as developed in the 1990s, was introduced. Genome Editing is a successor to the earlier GM approach. The wider issues associated with genetic modifications are discussed in Chapter 4.

The genetic modification of plants and micro-organisms in the 1990's raised significant issues.[99] Many of these concerns are extant and will impact on whether and to what extent Genome Editing comes to be used in this sector.[100] So, what were and are the key issues?

First, the GM debate demonstrated that the importance of food went beyond the simple role of producing nutrients for human consumption. In one sense this had long been a factor.[101] During the debate Government

---

98 Carey N (2020) *Hacking the Code of Life: How Gene Editing Will Rewrite our Futures*, Icon Books, London.

99 Avise JC (2004) *The Hope, Hype and Reality of Genetic Engineering*, OUP.

100 Bruce D and Bruce A (1998) *Engineering Genesis: The ethics of genetic engineering in non-human species*, Earthscan Publications Ltd, London.

101 Acts 10: 9-16.

focussed on convincing people that GM food was safe. However, for many, the concern was the concept of the importation of alien genes into food; fish genes into strawberries was an example that led to a sense of GM being 'unnatural' and to the reaction 'Yuk'. The official response was based on the view that if only people really understood things (as government and the biotechnology industry did) then these fears would evaporate. Major efforts were made to explain. This didn't work because the issue was cultural not intellectual. Similar issues underlie the attractiveness of 'Organic Food' for many.[102] This is a discussion about core values (as discussed in Chapter 4) and alternative visions of the world.[103] Views on such issues may be imperfectly expressed but they are real. For many they link to inherent core values.[104] All of these issues remain relevant.

Second was the impact upon the environment. This has dimensions ranging from impact on the design of cropping systems to concerns about the transfer of genes e.g. for resistance to a particular herbicide, to wild species That one of the crops being modified, oil seed rape, was a close relative of a number of weed species, such as charlock and shepherd's purse, made this a real possibility. As noted before all of this was happening around 30 years after the advent of Rachel Carson's *Silent Spring*. Continuing concerns about the impact of chemical crop protection on wild life especially farmland birds and wild flowers were reignited by a technology which seemed likely to increase the use of chemicals in agriculture and to make even more of the rural landscape 'silent'.

Third was the area of Safety. This was new technology and so like all new technologies there were risks. As the Covid19 outbreak has shown society is ambivalent about what risks are justified. Much discussion focused on whether potential benefits justified perceived risk. In addition, who received the benefit and who carried the risks? The first GM introductions benefited the producer but not the consumer. The risks however were with the consumer. That the GM modification was to facilitate agro-chemicals,

---

102 Ritchie P (2020) 'Framing and Farming: Putting organics into a societal context', pp. 33-44 in *The Science Beneath Organic Production*, ed. D Atkinson and CA Watson, Wiley, London.
103 Atkinson D and Watson CA (2020) 'Science and Organic Agriculture', pp. 1-24, *ibid*.
104 Atkinson D *et al* (2012) 'Food Security: A churches together approach', *Rural Theology* 10, 27-42.

such as Glyphosate[105] amplified safety concerns. It was completely unrelated, but for some, concerns took them back to the Thalidomide cases of the early 1960's and the unwillingness of government and manufacturers to act for those adversely impacted. This led into a debate on labelling and the questions around what delivered informed choice.

Fourth was the role of Science. Could Science be relied upon to make fundamental changes to something as critical to life as food? Did industry really have an appropriate level of understanding? GM technologies required the bringing together of genes from across the length of evolutionary time, genes which had not co-existed for millennia. Were we really sure that this was wise? These concerns were amplified by the Government's approach to providing support for the 'Science View' though the Polkinghorne Committee[106] which discussed the matter in the following way:

A key question can be refined as, is the *identity* of the gene from the originating organism transferred with it? Alternatively, is a gene simply a complex chemical which is transferred across species without ethical reservations? Essentially does DNA from a pig remain pig DNA if put into another species or is it just DNA. The Polkinghorne Committee placed stress on the original genetic material having been diluted to almost zero so that a recipient organism was unlikely to receive any material which had ever been in the donor organism. The transferred gene was merely a copy which might have been produced entirely through chemical synthesis and thus with no potential for moral taint.

Was this convincing at the time? No! Did it help the case? No! If genes make us who we are, then genes are part of our identity, and if a gene is moved to another organism then part of the donor's identity goes with it. If we are a product of our genes, then those genes must have a role in defining us.

Fifth was the Response of Government. The Government wanted GM introduced and took a pro-industry stand. They constantly reiterated that they were merely following the Science. However as discussed in Chapter 2, Science does not result in a single view. This is especially the case for the biological Sciences where much is probabilistic.

---

105 Grosbard E and Atkinson D (1985) *The Herbicide Glyphosate*, Butterworth, London.
106 MAFF (1993) Report on the ethics of Genetic modification and Food Use, HMSO, London.

Sixth was the Spiritual Dimension. If life is just a matter of biology and chemistry, and The Polkinghorne Report in its approach to genes tended in that direction,[107] then questions are asked about our relationship with God. The suggestion that we are all merely DNA multiplying machines, a survival mechanism for genes, is perhaps the ultimate reductionist take.[108] This issue is discussed again in Chapter 7.

The genetic modification of plants remains a live issue. Genome Editing techniques are being used to modify crop plants just as were GM techniques in the 1990's. Many of the ethical issues linked to plants also are issues in respect of animal products. Considering animals does bring the issues closer to ourselves.

Case studies

For much of our time on Earth, man has selectively bred animals to better meet our need for food and for other uses. Poultry may be bred for rapid meat production or for egg production, Cattle are bred for meat or for dairy products. Sheep are bred for meat production or for fibre production. This has increasingly been aided by emerging technologies linked to our understanding of genetics and our ability to manipulate an edited embryo into receptive females. The technology which underpins the gene editing of farm animals resembles that used to clone animals and which came to prominence with the birth of Dolly the Sheep in the 1990s.[109] Issues related to the use of Genome Editing in relation to farm animals were considered by the SEC's working group on Genome Editing and much of what is considered here is a product of those discussions.[110]

African Swine Fever (ASF). ASF is a devastating disease, which leads to pigs dying of catastrophic bleeding within ten days of infection. Currently no effective vaccine or treatment exists. It is spreading steadily across Europe from Asia. The standard response to outbreaks is a cull of all animals at risk of infection. In contrast to the domestic pig, the

---

107 MAFF (1993), *ibid.*

108 Dawkins R (1976) *The Selfish Gene*, OUP.

109 Carey N (2020) 'Editing the animal world', pp. 51-69.

110 Genome working Group of the Church and Society Committee of the SEC (2019) 'What it means to be human: the Challenge of Genome Editing'. Report to the 2019 General Synod of the Scottish Episcopal Church.

African Warthog appears to be tolerant to the virus. The Roslin Institute in Edinburgh identified a genetic variant in the warthog and have edited this gene into UK pigs. Modified pigs are being tested to see if they are tolerant to ASF. This could thus be seen as a modification to domestic pigs with the aim of improving animal health and a parallel to the issues discussed in Chapter 5. However much of the controversy about GM technology related to transgenesis, the transfer of a gene from one species to another. This would be an instance of transgenesis as African Warthogs and domestic pigs do not naturally interbreed.

Porcine reproductive and respiratory syndrome (PRRS). PRRS is a widespread serious infectious disease, leading to deaths of foetuses in pregnancy, and piglets born with severe respiratory symptoms, diarrhea and greater vulnerability to secondary bacterial infections. At a time when antibiotic use in livestock production is being strongly discouraged this potential use of Genome Editing is an alternative. Researchers at the Roslin Institute in Edinburgh have used Genome Editing to disable part of the protein which allows the PRRS virus to enters pig cells. This makes pigs resistant to the disease. The disease is both a concern for animal welfare and causes significant economic losses.

De-horning (polling) dairy cattle. Dairy cattle usually grow horns. It is common practice to de-horn calves soon after birth so as to prevent the cattle damaging each other or their handlers. This is an unpleasant process involving surgery or cauterisation. Dairy cows without horns have been created by editing – from a rare genetic variant found naturally in some beef cattle. To introduce the variant by selective breeding would take many years and could impact other breeding objectives. Genome Editing could do this quickly and might be considered as an animal welfare benefit. However, the motive for wanting to do this is both our convenience and a consequence of our production systems.

Golden Rice. Rice is a staple part of the diet for billions of people worldwide. It does not however meet all dietary needs[111]. It lacks vitamin A. Vitamin A is needed for the functioning of the immune system and for the functioning of sight. Significant numbers of children become blind each year as a result of vitamin A deficiency. Golden rice was engineered to express extra genes in rice seeds leading to the production of Beta-

---

111 Carey N (2020) 'Feed the world', pp. 33-50.

Carotene which is converted, in humans, to vitamin A. These genes do not come from within the rice genome. The new genes are transgenes. Research led to the quantities produced being increased to levels which seemed likely to have an effect. That this has not yet become available is blamed on organisations such as Greenpeace who believe that this whole technology and approach is fundamentally wrong and so consequential benefits are irrelevant. A number of key questions remain. Will the levels of Beta-carotene found in the modified rice have a real effect? Why have Biotech companies not gone ahead with its use in developing countries where there are no bars to the release of GM crops? Why is GM modified rice the only way of resolving a problem which in the rest of the world is dealt with by the consumption of a more varied diet?

Adam. In Genesis humanity's relationship with God is characterised by the metaphorical figure of Adam[112] who is given the task of naming the animals. In reflecting on this it is important to remember that Adam is a metaphor for humanity. We ought not to think of Adam as a person going round with a clip board and a pen and ticking off each genotype. There was a question as to what were distinctly different forms of animals, species in our terms. Adam also had a duty of care. We have assumed responsibility for the nature and the care of our domesticated animals. The use of Genome Editing for this purpose could seem to be consistent with this responsibility. There are however questions which link to whether the health changes which we might affect would have been needed had we reared or cared for the animals in a different way. A key question is perhaps: What is our motive for the Genome Editing?

In Genesis we read:

The Lord God formed a human being from the dust of the ground and breathed into his nostrils the breath of life, so he became a living creature. The Lord God took the man and put him into the Garden of Eden to till it and look after it. Then the Lord God said, 'It is not good for the man to be alone . . .' So, from the Earth he formed all the wild animals and all the birds of the air and brought them to the man to see what he would call them; whatever the man called each living creature, that would be its name. The man gave names to all cattle, to the birds of the air, and to every wild animal. (Genesis 2: 7, 15, 18-20)

---

112 This is discussed in detail in Chapter 2 and in Chapter 12 in the section on Evolution.

Is Genome Editing consistent with the charges given to Adam? Is transgenic Genome Editing comparable to Identity Theft?

The New Questions

Recently developed molecular techniques such as Genome Editing permit a wider range of fundamental changes to the genetics of an animal species. Things only speculated about, even in the relatively recent past, are either now possible or seem likely to become possible in the near future.[113] This raises new questions and makes it urgent to answer questions which have been with us for some time. Among the most demanding are:

How do we set the balance between our needs and the good of a companion species? How do we value other species?

Is it OK to modify basic features of ruminant animals because of issues linked to Climate Change, many of which are a consequence of our decisions on the life-style to which we have become accustomed?

Is it OK to add genes from other species? If it is, is this acceptability for genes from anywhere or just from closely related species?

Should we restrict the use of Genome Editing to changes linked to animal health?

So, what's different from the GM era? The key differences seem to be:

Genome Editing is more precise. The ballistic method, which was commonly used to create GM constructs, was 'shot gun' in both approach and consequences.

It does not have to have at its heart the import of material from other species. It can be used to repair what is there.

Many of the current animal applications differ from typical GM applications in being targeted at improving welfare and combating diseases.

Assessing Ethical Issues. Discussions of proposed actions and an improved understanding of where others had issues has, in the past, been helped by using the series of 'Gateway' questions developed by Michael Banner as part of his work on ethical issues in animal breeding.[114] These

---

113 Genome working Group of the Church and Society Committee of the SEC (2019) 'What it means to be human; The Challenge of Genome Editing'.

114 Anon (1995) Report of the committee to consider the ethical implications of emerging technologies in the breeding of farm animals, HMSO, London.

questions have over recent years been used as a format for examining a range of issues.[115] The procedure works by beginning with an inherent question and only moving to consequential questions if the more fundamental issues are not identified as insurmountable blockages.

First (an Inherent question): Is this a harm, which should never be permitted? Identifying the object or process of the questioning as such a harm ends the process. No further examination is needed. An example is the issue for some over the use of human embryos in research. If it is considered acceptable, at least in some cases, then examining consequential issues is the next step.

Second (a Consequential question): Do the expected benefits outweigh identified disbenefits by a substantial margin? Answering this cost-benefit question *positively* allows progression to the final question.

Third (another Consequential question): What can be done to mitigate some or all of the disbenefits?

These questions are relevant to all of the proposed issues in relation to the use of Genome Editing technologies for both humans and animals but, while humans may be able to engage in dialogue about potential uses in medicine, animals cannot.

Reflections and Questions. Animal breeding is a well-worked area for ethical questions.[116] SEC's working group on Genome Editing revisited some of these of which the most demanding were:[117]

First: Should we be making direct genetic interventions in another species

Second: Do the alterations made using Genome Editing differ from GM?

Third: How far and for what purposes we may use our new technical capacities to intervene in food animals?

---

115 Atkinson D (2009) 'Soil microbial resources and agricultural policies', pp. 1-16 in *Mycorrhizas, Functional Processes and Ecological Impact*, ed. C Azcon-Aguilar, JM Barea, S Gianinazzi and V Gianinazzi-Pearson, Springer, Berlin.

116 Anon (1995) Report of the committee to consider the ethical implications of emerging technologies in the breeding of farm animals.

117 Genome working Group of the Church and Society Committee of the SEC (2019) 'What it means to be human; The Challenge of Genome Editing'.

The history of societal objections to GM modifications indicated that there are societal concerns linked to the use of new technologies on animals and with the potential to change animal products. Concerns cover the spectrum from issues linked to animal rights to dietary issues which the current focus on veganism has re-raised in society as a whole. However, the two key underlying issues are <u>transgenesis</u> i.e. the addition of genetic material from another species and <u>naturalness</u>. The second is hard to define, but its links to our core values and identity make it nevertheless very real.

Genome Editing can modify the genome of an organism adding genes from another species. Creating a mutation in pigs to confer tolerance to African swine fever, involves the import of a gene from a close but different species. To what extent would we regard this as being genetically 'unnatural' is perhaps a defining question which tests our views on this issue? Creating pigs resistant to the PRRS virus raises rather different issues. It involves knocking out part of a gene so as to disable the pathway used by the virus to infect the animal. While the genome of the domestic pig is well known, it remains possible that this mutation could be present within the wider pig population. Hornless dairy cattle raise other issues about naturalness and our relationships with domesticated animals. Hornless cattle involve a mutation introduced by Genome Editing but using a gene which, although relatively rare, already exists within the species. As the mutation for hornlessness is uncommon it can be asked whether by removing horns we are changing the nature of cattle in a fundamental way?

A key consequential question is whether the types of changes discussed above are more acceptable because some are aimed at giving the animal protection from disease? It's here that the technology is most similar to its potential use in humans and thus most likely to be acceptable. However, this asks fundamental questions about the basis of our relationship with other forms of life. Once we domesticated animals from the wild, what did we then owe them in terms of good stewardship? Is it restricted to keeping them well looked after, protected from harms and not restricting their freedoms? Producing cattle without horns might be consistent with such practice. However, it can equally be argued that horn damage is exacerbated by intensive dairy production systems and that Genome Editing is a mere technical fix.

Conclusions

The question 'Is Genome Editing acceptable?' cannot be given a simple 'yes/no' answer. Each case will have distinct elements and will ask different questions. The case studies above illustrate the range of issues which may arise. Many were already being asked in respect of agricultural practices. What is now different is that the ease of the Genome Editing technology makes things possible for the first time, and puts long-standing questions in a new context.

The Bible lays down the principles and values by which we may make ethical judgements. Scripture explores how we are called to relate to other parts of the creation. At the beginning of our relationship with God, the 'metaphorical Adam' is given an individual name, 'Adam', and additionally the task of giving animals a name. Similarly, as soon as she was, Eve, received a name. Names have a close relationship to identity. Much of the book of Genesis is about identity. In it we see the establishment of identity for individuals such as the patriarchs. Through their identities we learn much about humanity and about our identity in partnership with God. The identity of a group of people, the people of Israel, is forged in the Genesis story. Does the message of Genesis go beyond mere classification? I'm tempted to add, Discuss.

Naming is important. Parents think long and hard about the names they give to their children. In the giving of names parents hope they are giving characteristics to their children. Family history can be preserved in a name. Names may identify an individual and make them distinct from others. This can be true of a family or some other group united by a particular set of characteristics. In giving names Adam had the job of classifying the living parts of God's creation. Classification is usually done on the basis of a group of distinct features, which are unique to that species. Individual features may be shared with members of other species. However, when we take features from one organism and transfer it to another, we take an element of identity and make the host species less distinct. The prospect of moving genes from one species to another thus asks some fundamental questions. The relationship of name and identity is further explored in Chapter 7.

What else might help? So many of the parables, the stories with a purpose, told by Jesus, relate to the production of food such as the parable of the sower, or to animal husbandry such as those related to the care of sheep. Issues linked to food clearly matter. What might we learn and what is relevant to the Genome Editing debate from the man who built a larger barn for his crops?

> *Jesus said, 'There was a rich man whose land yielded a good harvest. He debated with himself: "What am I to do? I have not the space to store my produce. This is what I will do," said he. "I will pull down my barns and build them bigger. I will collect in them all my grain and other goods . . ." But God said to him, "You fool, this very night you must surrender your life; and the money you have made, who will get it now?" That is how it is for the man who piles up treasure for himself and remains a pauper in the sight of God.'* (Luke 12: 16-21)

We began this chapter with a reflection on a rising world population and the challenges it poses. Many of our food production aims relate to producing more. If that feeds more people then that is good. If it is for financial gain then other issues come into play especially if there are externalities i.e. costs which are born by the environment or by other species as a consequence of the production system. The rich man could have made use of his surfeit of grain in many ways. He could have shared it with others but he elected to keep it for himself. The problem was his identification of his main priority. That can also apply to society. Why do we need to produce more? How does this relate to the viable capacity of our planet? Can we really justify increased production? Do these changes simply allow us to do something which, is in the long term, unsustainable? Questions which have been asked continually but which now have a new focus and perhaps an increased urgency. We will return to many of these issues in Chapter 10.

Chapter 7

Human Gender and Sexuality[118]

Genetics are important. The impact of genetics is at the heart of this volume. The effect of genetics is sometimes obvious and sometimes subtle. While we may share 50% of our genome with fruits like bananas the other 50% ensures that we are very unlike bananas. We share 98% of our genome with our Ape cousins but that 2% difference is responsible for major effects. We share a very high % of our genome with all our fellow humans but we cannot be unconscious of some of the differences which those very small differences occasion. Those with pink (white), black, Asian and minority ethnic appearance clearly look different. Male and female look different. In most of these aspects while the averages are different, we are aware that they represent a continuum. However, all of these things have attracted, over the time we have existed as a distinct species, a period of around 200,000 years, significant cultural associations which lead to differences in how things are done and perhaps to different roles.

When the human genome was sequenced in 2001[119] there were two major reactions. First, wonder that it had been successfully achieved. Second that it was so small, around 3 billion letters – Eukaryotic (plants and most animals) genomes can be as large as 100 billion letters – and that it contained lots of variation. Given the complexity of us as organisms, consensus expected our genome to be big. Perhaps it ought not to have been a surprise. When the structure of DNA was elucidated[120] there was surprise that it was as simple as four nucleotide bases working in combinations of three sets which coded for all the variety of proteins. However, it was that simple.

---

118 The underlying science for this chapter is detailed in Chapter 12 in the sections on Epigenetics, Evolution, DNA, the Human Genome and CRISPR.

119 Carey N (2020) *Hacking the Code of Life: How Gene Editing Will Rewrite our Futures*, Icon Books, London.

120 Doudna J and Sternberg SH (2017) *A Crack in Creation*, Bodley Head, London.

Following the elucidation of the human genome it then became clear that variation could be achieved through the agency of which genes were active in which tissues and at which times, the Science of Epigenetics.[121] As part of this it became clear that environmental factors, both the external environment and the environment in which a stem cell found itself, impacted behaviour. In this possibility might be found an explanation for things which up to that time had been a puzzle. These could vary from why cell replication sometimes went out of control (cancers) to why people, including identical twins, behaved differently. This understanding of functional genetics allows us to re-examine a whole range of things within our societies, including, perhaps, the expression of sexuality.

We have entitled this chapter gender and sexuality. Whether or not there is a real difference was a question addressed by a Church of England Group.[122] They defined *sex* as the biological reality which is experienced and expressed. They defined *gender* as the way this biological reality is experienced and expressed by individuals in social contexts. These definitions are relatively simplistic and would not be universally accepted. The definition and the interaction between these concepts form the basis of the problems which have challenged the church for decades.

This links us to issues related to the establishment of identity and the things which define us. These were discussed by Alister McGrath in a book which sought to link the establishment of identity within a wider human quest for meaning.[123] It's an issue for all of us during our teenage years. For some it can be a major struggle. In her autobiography, Rachel Mann, who was born male but became a woman, sets out the struggles she went through to establish what ought to be her true gender.[124] She concluded:

This is about the many faces of death. The focal point of dying is the loss of self and ultimately its recovery. At its heart this is a story about intangible and important things; it's about becoming who one is called

121   Carey N (2012) *The Epigenetics Revolution*, Icon Books, London; Francis RC (2011) *Epigenetics, how environment shapes our genes*, Norton, New York.

122   Davie M (2018) *Glorify God in your Body*, Lost Coin Books, London.

123   McGrath A (2017) *The Great Mystery: Science God, and the Human Quest for Meaning*, Hodder and Stoughton, London.

124   Mann R (2012) *Dazzling Darkness: Gender, sexuality, illness and God*, Wild Goose Publications, Glasgow.

to be. And its conclusion is that finally we are simply called to be ourselves. The only and somewhat frustrating problem is that for us as humans to be ourselves is a tricky business. A tree gives glory to God by being a tree. For humans we have so many possibilities. And so, the only way any of us can know and be truly ourselves is to know ourselves in God.

Why has sexuality been so important to so many at various times in human history? Why does it seem to have been so important to many in our churches? Why have a small number of references in a limited part of Scripture had such an impact?

In reviewing fundamental issues in relation to health and society, John Wyatt commented on the unparalleled success of scientific reductionism as applied to human biology[125] – its understanding, all that makes us what we are, from our basic genetic coding. Elsewhere in this book I have referred to the suggestion made by Richard Dawkins[126] that we are merely survival machines, robots programmed to preserve selfish molecules known as genes. Seen in this way all of life is part of a machine aimed at replicating DNA. In some ways our DNA, and that of most other living organisms, works rather like a sophisticated virus with a total emphasis on replication. We are all machines, built by DNA and whose purpose is to make more copies of the same DNA. We exist merely to spread 'copy me' programmes. If this is the case then those who elect not to reproduce, not to respond to the 'copy me' command, will not sit easily within this inherent DNA plan and within society.

We can use this thought to examine the guidance of Scripture. Perhaps the most important question is why is sexuality seen as being so defining of an individual? What is so very wrong about same sex relationships that the subject has resulted in such division within and between churches in our time?

Beginning a Story

A key question is whether recent discoveries in Science can both provide a basis of explanation for same sex relationships and consequently a way for churches to genuinely open up discussion of this issue both

125 Wyatt J (2009) *Matters of Life and Death*, Intervarsity Press, London.
126 Dawkins R (1976) *The Selfish Gene*, OUP.

within themselves and with society. Common observation and history tell us that not every individual is born totally and unequivocally either male or female. The rise of the LGBT (Lesbian, Gay, Bisexual and Transsexual) movement has made this both clearer and a significant issue for today. Male and female may represent modes (peaks) on a spectrum but patently there is variation around and across those modes. Modern scientific knowledge and Scripture can point in different directions. Knowledge of the developing Sciences of epigenetics and of neural development help us understand the causes of variation in sexuality and even suggest a possible mechanism by which variation in sexuality may be brought about. This may help. How we incorporate this into our relationship with those who express as LGBT will, in this book, revolve around shoes and an accident and will continue the journey through the challenges in today's world of developing bioscience.

History is the story of our past. Attitudes to homosexuality do not make happy reading. It has taken years for attitudes to change and so to allow gay people to be themselves and have pride in who they are and what they feel. It's ironic that many of them, from all backgrounds and professions, tell of experiences that one of the places they felt least welcome and accepted, was in the Church The following are two factual cases from our time, centred on identity.

2003 Rachel Mann, now an Anglican parish priest, recalls that during the period leading up to her candidacy, training and Ordination she was advised by some sympathetic clergy that she should refrain from disclosing that she was gay and in a same sex relationship! She still is gay but now able to be open about it.

2020 Father Azariah France-Williams is about to have his latest book published: *Ghost Ship: Institutional Racism and the Church of England*. Ten years on from his Ordination he describes how as a black priest he felt invisible and ignored, but now with the current raised awareness of blatant BAME discrimination and inequalities, he's quoted as saying that during the past few weeks he feels that some of his white friends and colleagues are starting to listen to him, and also that a number of them have contacted him to apologise for the times they've been complicit!

Case Studies

Shoes and an Accident. As an introduction to this section, Margaret provided the first paragraph. It's a Case Study, not about some fictional person, but one that is about you, me, everyone!

An old Eskimo proverb says we should not judge others and their actions till we have walked a mile in their *shoes*. We all only know what we know of life from walking in our own shoes. As we have walked the many, many miles on our own particular life's journey, we have made choices and decisions with varying successful or otherwise outcomes. However, we did not make the one choice or decision that had a total effect on our lives. We had no part in it. It was an *accident* in the true meaning of that word – it just happened. *We were born.* We had no choice in terms of who our parents would be – Caucasian? Ethnic? Caring? We had no choice as to where geographically we would be born – UK? Pakistan? Timbuktu? These two accidents of birth have tangible obvious features and consequences. But alongside these there is one other predominant consequence that we can't discern in detail by looking at someone or at ourselves – and that is the genetic package with which we came into the world!

Our understanding of the complexities and mysteries of this genetic package and its effect on our lives is far advanced today from what it was even 10, or 15 years ago, let alone many decades or centuries ago. As touched on earlier in this book our knowledge of genetics and gene editing is having beneficial effects on countless lives in terms of improved life conditions and disease prevention. It is easy for us to discern some basic genetic characteristics in this package we each have e.g. Blue eyes/ brown hair, but it's now acknowledged that much to do with our sexuality/ sexual orientation comes as part of this total package too.

It is this last genetic fact that causes endless concern among certain Christians. To many, God created man and woman in his image and their role in life was to go forth and multiply – end of story. Two genders, no in-betweens. However, we now know this is not how it really is. Alongside gender discrimination, another form of it relates to BAME people. Discrimination varies from total to zero and many degrees in between, and is currently a real focus of concern. These variations of acceptance have long had a detrimental effect on all those who have felt rejected, misunderstood, unaccepted by the world around them – be they family /society /the Church of many denominations. For each of us our birth was not under our control nor was the genetic and epigenetic package we came with.

Therefore, to return to the Eskimo proverb we know how we have progressed through life in our own shoes but we haven't made that journey in anyone else's shoes – so why have so many in our world been made to suffer as a result of their *designated* sexual/ethnic package? Can Christians justify prejudice by reference to Bible quotations? Is there evidence that sexual orientation or skin colour should have a hierarchical scale of acceptance?

Al and Bo. Consider the case of two brothers who had both reached the age of 20.[127] Al was normal for his age. Bo was pre-adolescent with poorly developed muscles and no facial hair. A medical inspection revealed that Bo had vestigial genitals He was suffering from Kallmann Syndrome, a disorder of sexual development. This was strange because Al and Bo were born as identical twins. What happened to Bo that didn't happen to Al? Kallmann Syndrome affects sexual development and the sense of smell. Kallmann impacts the olfactory placode in the brain. Smell begins here but so do the neurones, which migrate to the hypothalamus and which impact sexual development. Al like Bo had an impaired olfactory development. Kallmann Syndrome is a genetic linked disease, but Al and Bo had, as identical twins, identical genetics. Their differences were due to epigenetics. Epigenetics refer to long-term alterations of DNA, which do not involve changes in the DNA sequence itself. Either Al's DNA was epigenetically modified so as to ameliorate his Kallmann expression or Bo's was altered in a way which exacerbated it.

The Dutch Hunger Winter. Audrey Hepburn was one of the 20th Century's most admired film stars.[128] However, her beauty, bone structure and petiteness was the result of great hardship. She was a product of what is known as the Dutch Hunger Winter, which lasted from November 1944 until late spring 1945. A German blockade resulted in a chronic shortage of the quantity of food available to the Dutch population. The population had to survive on 30% of normal calorific intake resulting in people eating grass

---

127 Francis RC (2011) *Epigenetics*, Norton, New York.
128 Carey N (2012).

and tulip bulbs. The survivors were a well-defined group of people who had all suffered one period of acute malnutrition and at the same time.

Records allowed this group or cohort to be traced and for the effects of the starvation to be followed. This was so for children born during or immediately subsequent to the period. If the mother was well fed around the time of conception and malnourished for only the final period of pregnancy the baby was likely to be born small. If the mother was malnourished for the first three months of pregnancy and was then well fed the baby was likely to be born with a normal birth weight. Following up on these babies it became clear that the small babies stayed small for most of their lives and had reduced rates of obesity even though they had normal access to food for most of their lives. Why were these children not able to revert when well fed? Children whose mothers had been malnourished during early pregnancy however had increased rates of obesity. There were also impacts on mental health.

Clearly events which happen in the early weeks of pregnancy can have a lasting impact. Some of these effects were passed on to grandchildren. This is a result of molecular epigenetic effects, which result in impaired developmental programming and lifelong defects in gene expression and in cellular functioning. During early development it seems likely that epigenetic proteins are essential to the stabilising of gene expression patterns. These can become set and transmitted to daughter cells or maintained in cells such as neurones, which can last for decades. Because the epigenome gets stuck so too are the patterns of expression. I will come back to this later.

Jonathan. Where might we look in the Bible for help? The issues around sexuality get rather little coverage. I begin by looking at Jonathan, son of King Saul and friend of David who was to be Saul's successor as King.

What can we learn from and about Jonathan? In the Books of Samuel, we read:

When Saul had talking with David, he kept him and would not let him return any ore to his father's house, for he saw that Jonathan had given his heart to David and had grown to love him as himself. (1 Samuel 18: 1-2)

I grieve for you, Jonathan my brother; you were most dear to me; your love for me was wonderful, surpassing the love of women. (2 Samuel 1: 26)

Was the relationship between David and Jonathan a homosexual one? It has been suggested,[129] but we will never know. There is however a more important point than his sexuality. What is clear is that this was a close and loving relationship. From Scripture we know so much more about Jonathan. Whether or not he was gay, what is clear is that he was unequivocally *not* defined by his sexuality. He was defined by many things. He was defined by his prowess as a warrior, as the King's son and by a range of other characteristics. It matters to get things into perspective. It is these things which define us, and which ought to have the greatest influence on our place in community and society. Our Saviour's reactions to people emphasises this.

Issues Raised

Understandings from Epigenetics.   Most of our features depend upon our genetic makeup. We understand the chromosomal difference which results in people being either 'Male' or 'Female'. The genetic basis of this is relatively clear. Sexuality and perceived gender are much more complex and far less clear. On the basis that there is no single gene nor a simple basis in genetics that might be responsible for sexuality, it has been suggested that homosexuality must just be a lifestyle choice. This is an over simplistic take on genetics. Consider cell development. Every one of our cells has the same genetic makeup but not all of our cells end up being identical. Skin cells, nerve cells, muscle cells, heart cells, liver cells are all very different yet they all have the same DNA. How did this happen? This is a very deep question which illustrates what we understand and where we still marvel. Think about your fingerprints. We all have them. They are different between each individual hence their use in criminology. They differ from our parents and our sibling's prints. If we damage our fingers the skin re-grows and with the same fingerprint. The same genetic code dictates that cells produced from skin stem cells will continue to produce skin cells and, on the fingers, will produce a distinctive ridged pattern. The mechanism we understand in general terms, but the mechanistic detail not yet. We still have much to learn.

---

129 Sharpe K (2011) *The Gay Gospels: Good News for Lesbian, Gay, Bisexual and Transgender People*, O Books, Alresford, Hants.

Could epigenetic mechanisms have a role in the much more complex area of gender definition? Does neural development have a role in this? Does the pattern of hormone production have a defining role? Hormones are proteins coded for by genes. Production varies between the sexes and with age, and is impacted by environment, so there is scope for many different outcomes.

It can help us when thinking of such issues to think of a parallel in literature. Think of *Romeo and Juliet*, Shakespeare's play. It has been filmed many times. It has been performed on stage even more times. Were all performances identical even though they were using the same script? No, it is clear that the same script, even the same words but with different voices and pace can result in a very different end product.

The 'naked gene' consists of DNA as a double helix. The functioning of that DNA is, however, modified by other chemicals which are both an integral part of the gene and are able alter the behaviour of the gene. Epigenetics can make genes more or less active. Epigenetic pathways are important throughout life, but are particularly significant during early development. They are the basis of the interaction of the genetic code with environment, the nurture factor. This allows sophisticated fine tuning of gene expression. Is it the basis of differences in sexuality and its expression? Is it the basis for the disjuncture of sex and gender? It seems a possible explanation. It certainly provides enough of a feasible and viable explanation to be part of the discussion.

If we return to Al and Bo it is unclear what caused that epigenetic shift. We know that epigenetic changes can occur in the womb. Al and Bo shared a womb, but even for identical twins, commonly one becomes dominant. Knowledge of epigenetics is currently increasing due to its role in our understanding of cancer. Our parents make separate and equal genetic contributions to who we are, but they make unequal epigenetic contributions. Some genes are active if received from the mother but inactive if from the father. Other epigenetic states are transmitted from grandparents. Hence there is complexity. The complete answer to the question of sexuality? No, but certainly something to reflect upon.

Where does Scripture come in?   Sexuality is a broad topic; same sex relationships continue to fuel debate among Christians. When Parliament legislated to make same sex marriage possible this presented a challenge to the churches. Other sexuality-linked issues raised by LGBT people are also relevant. As with issues around the beginning of life, which were discussed in Chapter 5, debate among church attenders tends to come down to scriptural interpretation.

The Ten Commandments[130] provide broad principles guiding us how life ought to be lived. Jesus (citing the Old Testament) reduced even these to 'Love God, love people'. However, the Jewish people at the time of Moses wanted more detail and much more specific guidance. Leviticus (and Deuteronomy) provided this for a range of topics including a number related to sexual relationships. Key to the underlying theme of this Chapter and at the core of the stated problem for churches are the following two verses:

You must not lie with a man as with a woman.[131]

If a man has intercourse with a man as with a woman, both commit an abomination.[132]

In terms of Scripture and in relation to specific rather than inferred guidance, that's it. This particular issue is not raised in Deuteronomy. Why has this been so much more important for many in our churches than almost any other two single verses? Even in relation to Leviticus, it is important to note that many other sexual practices such as having intercourse with someone else's wife, a daughter-in-law, an aunt, a stepmother or step-sister and a wide range of non sex-related issues are condemned in similar terms.

It is clear from the scriptural books of that era that the people of Israel were perpetually at war with other tribes. The land of milk and honey to which they moved was not an unpopulated area. It was heavily populated and the Israelites had to fight for survival. Producing men for the army mattered to establish the Israelites place on their land. If we return to Richard Dawkins' thoughts on DNA[133] – were those who mis-used the sexual act in this 'abominating' way failing to follow the 'copy me' directive

---

130 Deuteronomy 5: 7-21.

131 Leviticus 18: 22.

132 Leviticus 20: 13.

133 Dawkins R (1976).

and in doing so were reducing the potential number of fighting men? It's another of those 'Discuss' questions. A thought.

While many of the non-traditional sexual practices identified above may be regarded as undesirable, they do not attract condemnation in the same way as do same-sex relationships. However, it's clear that passages in Scripture relating to homosexuality[134] are relatively rare:[135] hatred is mentioned 21 times, lying and false testimony 30, greed, avarice and covetousness 40, theft 42, adultery 52, murder 57, self-righteousness 79, and idolatry 169 times!

Within the church there have been three principal reactions to this issue:

First, that Scripture clearly condemns homosexuals, or

Second, that Scripture condemns homosexuality, not homosexuals. Christians are called upon to hate the sin but love the sinner or

Third, that all these passages must be interpreted according to their contexts. Considering context can result in a very different interpretation. Few of the texts bear directly on the issue of sexuality but have been assembled to provide support for a position with a basis elsewhere. When read in context Bible passages can have a range of potential meanings!

Conclusions

There are challenges to the myriad of issues around human sexuality. These are informed by attitudes to and the experiences of the many people in the LGBT community; those who are openly gay or lesbian or transgender or want to change gender – even children, those who live feeling unhappy in their sexuality but are hiding it. As we address these challenges, early in 2020, a well-known TV personality has recently spoken movingly of his struggles to come to terms with his homosexuality – but feeling the time had come to 'come-out'; despite being happily married for 27 years and the father of 2 grown up daughters, he needed to be honest with himself and those he loved. 'Coming-out' is never easy. Whilst he

---

134 Homosexuality is explicitly mentioned in only seven Bible Passages: Genesis 19: 4-11, Judges 19: 22-24, Leviticus 18: 22, 20: 13, Romans 1: 26-27, 1 Corinthians 6: 7-11, 1 Timothy 1: 8-11.

135 Irvine Carl (2019) Sexuality Discussion Paper prepared for the Church of Scotland and used in a presentation in Kintore Parish Church.

is but one of countless people who have gone through similar stress and mental anguish, his open and public revelation will have been greeted with surprise, shock and yes, disgust by some.

Down the decades all these attitudes will have been expressed in varying degrees depending on the cultures, faiths and traditions that individuals are born into and live among. Experiencing such, often hostile, attitudes leads to there being many people who will have chosen to go through a life which is consistent with how they 'look', but a life they know is not how they truly feel inside i.e. they live concealing their 'real self'. Focussing on our faith as Christians how do we collectively and individually react to people in the LGBT community? Do we welcome them? Treat them like ourselves? Discriminate against them? What is life like in their shoes?

That our sexual orientation is innate is the conclusion of many in society including most of the LGBT community. It is still not universally accepted in churches. Bear in mind our premise at the outset of this discussion that everyone comes into the world through the circumstances of their parents and their place of birth – and that these two factors combine to subject each of us to exposure to certain cultural and faith experiences, traditions and expectations over which we have no choice – until at such times we are of an age to make individual choices and decisions about some aspects of our lives. Attitudes to sexuality and sexual practice have a long and varied history. We can read how things have changed over the years. The concept of the nuclear family is only one form of households today. What determines what is the best way to bring up children? What proof is there that two loving Mums, or two loving Dads, provide a less good family set up?

Even if a person has had long held beliefs that homosexuality is wrong, would that change if one of their children turned out to be gay? Would acceptance and love for that child and hopes for their happiness in life overcome their prejudice or their interpretation of their faith and its teachings? For many this is challenging to accept. In general, the young have less of a problem with what they regard as the new norms. So where does that place the Church and those of us as defined Christians? Not that many decades ago mixed-race relationships and marriages were similarly disapproved of. If we are all created equal in God's eyes, do we accept that different skin colour can indicate levels of superiority? Again, if we are all created equal in God's eyes, are people who are in the LGBT community lesser beings? Where does Christianity stand on these issues? Is it a generational thing? What would we do, feel, expect if we were wearing these *different* shoes?

Human sexuality is a fundamental issue and challenge because it is about who and why we are and why each one of us is walking in our shoes. What can we learn from our Saviour's teaching on relationships? The basis of much Christian teaching on issues related to sexuality and gender is taken from Jesus's answer to the Pharisees *when asked about divorce*:

> *In the beginning, the Creator made them male and female. That is why a man leaves his father and mother and is united to his wife, and the two become one flesh. It follows that they are no longer two individuals: they are one flesh.*[136]

This is a statement about heterosexual marriage and **not** about sexuality or gender. It depends upon a literal reading of at least some of Chapters 1-3 of Genesis, an issue we discuss in detail in Chapter 2. There is of course also a question as to whether the Gospel story about the healing of the servant of the centurion was the healing of someone in a long term committed gay relationship?[137] The social imbalance between the centurion and his servant was so unequal that it raises this as a possibility.[138] More material for reflection?

In a number of places in this book, Job has been used as an example of the role of Wisdom Literature. This can impact upon how the concept of the absolute nature of a *genetic basis* to sexual development is viewed. In Job's conversation with God, God says to Job:

> *But consider the chief of beasts, the crocodile, who devours cattle as if they were grass.*[139]

This is relevant here because it is not possible to predict the sex of a crocodile from its genetics. The sex of a crocodile depends upon the temperature at which the egg is hatched. The same blueprint can produce either a

---

136 Matthew 19:4-5, Mark 10: 6-7.

137 Sharpe K (2011) *The Gay Gospels: Good News for Lesbian, Gay, Bisexual and Transgender People.*

138 Matthew 8: 5-13; Luke 7: 1-10.

139 Job 40: 15.

male or a female. Hormone signalling is involved. Given the potential impact of Climate Change on temperatures this is of concern. It has been speculated that such effects contributed to the extinction of the dinosaurs – near relatives of crocodiles. Epigenetic modifications seem likely to be responsible for establishing or stabilising gender specific patterns of gene expression.[140]

Lastly, those of us of a certain age will recognise the 3Rs as fundamental in early education and so how about a new 3Rs in relation to sexuality and relationships?

Straight or Gay: how about if all relationships and our attitude to them were based on *Respect, Rights and Responsibilities*[141] – would that not result in universal acceptance of the equality of us all?

---

140 Carey N (2012).

141 Murison M (1986) *Respect, Rights and Responsibilities*, Westhill Academy Course Book.

Chapter 8

Where Does This Take Us?

Where to next? What new futures are possible? In this book I have examined the potential for using new biological technologies such as Genome Editing to influence the health and other features of ourselves and farm animals. Genome Editing's potential to treat or eliminate some human diseases and genetically linked defects has been explored. This led to questions about the ways in which we express our humanity and end of life issues. Together they question 'what it means to be human'. For Christians it asks how Science can inform our journey with Scripture. History shows that the most common response of the churches to scientific developments has been opposition. This has often left the church out of line with society and struggling to catch up. Developments in the biological Sciences seem likely to continue at an increasing rate. Knowledge of genetics and of epigenetics are expanding at a pace that means many visions of Science Fiction are becoming a new reality.

Where to next? Human enhancement is not a new concept. It is alive and well in many areas of life. Its vision dominates advertising for cosmetic products. It has become linked to Science and most visibly, in athletics and other sports. Sport Science has resulted in real gains in understanding of both what superior performances – in running, swimming, throwing, jumping, lifting weights etc – require from technique and their relationship to the human body. Pharmaceuticals have been developed to help and are commonly in an arms race with regulators as to what is or isn't allowed and what can be tested for. Blood supply can be augmented by pre-event transfusions. The aspiration for enhancement is alive and well. It is certain that this will continue and be augmented by increasing knowledge of genetic and epigenetic control of things currently only possible through chemistry. And that is before we begin to consider what might be better as a result of better understanding and control of neural and cerebral development. In addition, there are related developments focused on other species but again driven by our needs.

The re-emergence of Eugenics. Eugenics was a UK invention. The name was coined, in 1883 by Sir Francis Dalton, part of the Darwin family. He was concerned that advances in health care and welfare had sullied the national gene pool as a result of the sick and disabled being able to lead normal family lives.[142] It is reported that in 1912 the Spectator magazine commented on the issue in the following terms: 'The only way of cutting off the constant stream of idiots and feeble-minded individuals is to prevent those who are known to be mentally defective from producing offspring.'[143]

This was seen as coming from a belief in Science, rationalism, and being liberated from religious qualms. Recently it has even been suggested that the next couple of generations may be the last to accept pot luck with procreation. The views of Andrew Sabisky, a Government Advisor, and those of the current Prime Minister's principal Advisor, Dominic Cummings, on Eugenics, which recently featured in the Press, has brought the issue back into public debate.[144]

At the heart of thinking on Eugenics is a vision of improving humanity. Mr Sabisky had suggested links between race and intelligence and the desirability of limiting the breeding of the economically disadvantaged. In addition, he and Mr Cummings suggested that we move to selecting embryos/babies for higher IQ as part of the remit of the NHS so that these technologies should be available to all rather than just to the rich. This suggestion was based on the concept of selecting embryos with the best probability of having high intelligence. It was suggested that rich people already had the option of using IVF and selection of the egg that seemed most likely to produce the best option. Ideas for 'improving' humans were based on current approaches to animal breeding (Chapter 6). Approaches are linked to the notion that there are links between genes and intelligence i.e. that there are effectively 'intelligence genes'. This is all a vision for the future. That it is being promulgated by the senior Advisor to the PM suggests that we do need to think about it. How might the church react to the practice?

142 Fraser Nelson 2016 'Eugenics is back' pp. 12-13, Spectator, 2 April 2016.
143 The Spectator, 25 May 1912.
144 Greely A (2016) 'The end of sex', quoted in Mason R and Sample I (2020); Cummings supported selecting embryos for IQ pp. 1-2 in *The Guardian*, 20th February 2020.

Other issues asking questions. There are a range of other issues, which question the nature of humanity. Artificial Intelligence (AI) and robotics have questioned our role in a range of previously human activities. AI also asks questions about necessary skill levels, employment status and remuneration. Linked issues include the transfer of surgical procedures from consultant surgeons to nurses, the move of care homes from the UK to the far East so as to reduce care costs, the reduction in the mean age at death in the north of the UK linked to reduced employment and support payments. Could AI aid the use of technologies like CRISPR by reducing its cost? These are not all caused by biotechnology developments, but they are linked!

Where might we like to go? All that's been considered so far deals with humans as we are. Genome Editing however opens up options, which could result in humans being enhanced, in some form of directed and targeted evolution of humankind. New genetic methodologies such as Genome Editing and epigenetic modifications open up the possibility of accelerating human evolution by enhancing features such as musculature and thus perhaps strength or speed, or introducing novel approaches to resisting diseases. How wise would it be to use Genome Editing to modify people for non-medical reasons? Would it be acceptable to modify embryos in this way? These have become very real questions which need to be explored.

The immediacy of the issue. Our consideration of the use of CRISPR technologies on humans (Chapter 5) asked why society and individual Christians should be interested in Genome Editing? The conclusion was that these developments could change the whole nature of answers to the question 'what does it mean to be human.' In addition, new scientific techniques to manipulate the very genetic structure of humans (and other living things) could change our lives and those of people yet to be born. Some changes could be welcome, like therapies to treat hitherto incurable diseases. Other developments like creating genetically altered children posed profound ethical questions. The widely criticised birth of two gene edited children in China late last year moved things that had been visions of Science Fiction abruptly into today's reality.

The Birth of the First Genome Edited Children

This issue was visited in Chapter 5. It presents a vision of the future and so it seems appropriate to revisit the CRISPR Bombshell and its implications. At a conference held in November 2018 in Hong Kong on the subject of Human Genome Editing, a Chinese Scientist, So He Jiankui, reported the birth of two genome-edited babies. He had used CRISPR technology to modify human embryos. The babies had been modified to be resistant to HIV, a virus. The 8th December 2018 issue of the 'New Scientist' carried a picture of an 'enhanced baby' and the legend 'Welcome to a New Age of Humanity'. This was expanded in the coverage.[145] The Editorial lead was entitled 'Rewriting our future'. It concluded:

> We humans have been shaping our own evolution for millions of years through changes in the way we live, eat and reproduce. Until now such adaptation has depended on the random nature of evolution taking thousands of years. The CRISPR gene editing method has the potential to change all of that, giving us the power to fully take the reins of our genetic destiny and at speed. Last week He Jianku announced that he had created the first gene edited babies using CRISPR to alter a gene in human embryos. Now that we have crossed this line so casually, it is clear that careful regulation of such technologies is required. But perhaps the greatest danger is that editing genes using CRISPR is so easy.

The same issue of *New Scientist* speculated as to where this might take us.[146] It pointed out that the birth of Louise Brown, the first test tube baby, in 1978, had now been followed by around 8 million others and asked, can we now expect a similar opening of the flood gates? What is clear is that there is a clear division between those who would like to see germline editing research banned and those who see it as a way of preventing disease. New Scientist concluded:

> We all have thousands of harmful mutations that make us more prone to cancer, heart attacks or dementia. In principle everyone could live longer, healthier lives if these were repaired but we are still a long way from achieving this.

---

145 Special report: First gene edited babies, pp. 5-9, *New Scientist*, 8 December 2018.
146 Wilson C (2018) 'A Brave New World', pp. 8-9, *ibid.*

The inventors of the CRISPR technology[147] however, raised concerns about the use of the technology on human embryos and its implications if used to modify the human germline as this would be the first-time unborn humans had been subject to gene editing. Other commentators[148] expressed worries but suggested that the problem might not be so serious. Concerns around germline editing have focused on its use to produce super humans, people who are faster or even just more attractive. However, we currently understand little about the genetic basis of traits such as these and what we know suggests that changing complex features will be difficult because they are impacted by many genes. Wisdom Literature counsels, 'take care'. The history of new technologies asks, is this wise? It may also ask, is this a direction in which we want to go at all?

Other species. Genome Editing[149] is being used not only to impact the treatment of genetically based human diseases and elements of our food supply, but also on microbes to aid the production of pharmaceuticals, agrochemicals and other industrial chemicals. Yeast *Saccharomyces cerevisiae* has been genetically modified so as to produce cannabinoid compounds, Bacteria such as *E. coli* have been modified to produce drugs such as those related to violacein, a natural bactericide for use against Malaria. Some of these approaches involve the production of synthetic DNA and modifications to the bacterial genome by a reduction in the number of genes, from around 4,000 to as few as 799, so that it becomes focused on the production of the target product. Genome technologies are no longer restricted to existing genes; it is now possible to synthesise new genes and to implant them in target organisms. Would this pose dangers to existing microbes? Escape into and survival in the wild would be precluded, we are told, by building in a need for some specific nutrients unlikely to be found in the wild. Parallel questions were raised in the GM era. Gene transfer then as now involved the risk of genes moving to other than their intended home. GM Oil Seed Rape seeds were lost in transfer from field to factory resulting in plants growing wild and so with the

---

147 Doudna J and Sternberg SH (2017) *A Crack in Creation*, Bodley Head, London.
148 Carey N (2020) *Hacking the Code of Life: How Gene Editing Will Rewrite our Futures*, Icon Books, London.
149 King A (2020) 'Rewriting Biology', pp. 22-25 in *Chemistry and Industry*, July 2020, SCI, London.

opportunity to transfer genes to wild species of related genera. During the digestive process in animals, including ourselves, DNA fragments are liberated and can be assimilated into the genome of gut bacteria which can then be released in a transformed state to the environment. Containment is hard. This is a lesson from Covid19 and much of bacteriology.

In addition, there are wider ethical questions relating to our rights and responsibilities to other living things. Michael Jewett of North West University, Illinois said:

We end up with this tug of war between what cells want to do guided by their own evolutionary history and what we as engineers want.

Animal Use. As a species we have used animals for food and other purposes throughout recorded history. We have bred animals to enhance characteristics, which better suited them to our purposes. The public has in general accepted this as OK. (Chapter 6). Genome Editing using technologies like CRISPR now allows changes to be made in the genetics of farm animals to further enhance their food-linked characteristics. The same technologies however allow a wider range of changes. It's important to ask whether these are also acceptable or whether they cross a red line.

Challenging issues arise from Genome Editing of pigs to make their hearts and other organs more biologically compatible for potential transplant into humans, or to grow human tissues, such as a pancreas inside the pig.[150] Genome edited pig hearts have been successfully transplanted into baboons. The modified monkeys lived for at least 90 days suggesting a move to human clinical trials in the near future. The hope is that pig organs could help fill the gap in the number of organs available for transplant from human donors. The hearts used had been modified to produce human proteins and to block carbohydrates present in pigs, but absent in humans, so as to reduce the risk of organ rejection. Beyond the genetics there was need to develop the transplantation technology. Blood needed to be pumped through the heart throughout the whole procedure. The growth of the heart needed to be regulated, as the genes influencing heart growth continued to be active and with the aim of growing the size of heart needed for an adult pig rather

---

150 Whyte C (2018) 'A step closer to pig organs for people', pp. 10 in *New Scientist*, 8 December 2018.

than a much smaller monkey. In addition, there remain issues linked to the introduction of micro-organisms to which pigs but not humans have become adapted. Developments of this type ask questions about its acceptability but also illustrate some of the practical hurdles, which would be associated with a move from concept to practice.

Crops. Crops were at the heart of the GM debate of the 1990s and the use of Genome Editing for crop 'improvement' continues to arouse interest and provoke antagonism. These responses were the subject of a recent BBC Radio Programme which discussed how developments in plant science might both help to feed a growing world population and help adjustment to climatic changes.[151] Molecular approaches, such as Genome Editing, are helping develop understanding of basic processes in plants such as signalling, conversations happening within the crop plant. The ability to modify crop genomes, an aspiration at the heart of both many approaches to increasing production and of developing crop plants better attuned to the more variable conditions associated with Climate Change, remain key targets. Earlier in the book I commented that whilst whether a particular cropping system produced 10 tonnes of wheat per hectare or only 9 was important to a world with a rising population, it was not the only matter of importance. This remains true in relation to the ways in which Genome Editing might be used to enhance crops. The role of modified genetics has the potential to go beyond yields and has prospects for improved quality such as through increasing the content of micro-nutrients in the endosperm of seeds and thus through the potential to produce healthier flours and grains like white rice.

Job. Scripture cannot give us detailed guidance on the acceptability of such developments in Science. It does tell us much about being human. Our challenge is to link scriptural teaching on the nature of humanity to where the Science might lead us. The Wisdom Literature has been doing this for some time. Are we yet wise enough to make decisions with long term implications, where there is no option of turning back the clock were it to go wrong? Job has often been an early stop in any quest for

---

151 'The Life Scientific', BBC Radio 4, 18 August 2020. Professor Dale Saunders, Director of the John Innes Centre talked to Jim Al Khalili about how plant science might help to feed the world as the global population grows and how we respond to climate change.

wisdom especially when discussion of links between Science and faith are involved.[152]

These sentiments are reflected in the discussions between Job and God in Chapters 38-42 of the book. Many of the questions asked by God of Job are relevant in the context of current discussions as to whether we have the wisdom to modify the climate of our planet, to modify the animals with whom we share the planet and most particularly whether we have the understanding to modify the human genome in a way that cannot easily be reversed. God answered Job out of the storm, and said to him,

I shall put questions to you, and you must answer.[153]

There were profound environmental questions:

Where were you when I laid the earth's foundations? Tell me if you know and understand . . . Who supported the sea at its birth, when it burst in flood from the womb? . . . Have you visited the storehouse of the snow? . . . By what paths is the heat spread abroad? . . . Who has cut channels for the downpour?[154]

Questions concerning other species:

Can you hunt prey for the lioness and satisfy the hunger of young lions?[155]

The Lord then asked Job, 'Is it for a man who disputes with the Almighty to be stubborn? Should he who argues with God answer back?' Job answered the Lord, 'What reply can I give you, I who carry no weight? . . . I know that you can do all things and that no purpose is beyond you.'[156]

Issues Raised

The widely criticised birth of the two gene edited children in China late last year moved things that had been visions of Science Fiction abruptly into today's reality. The time for the society and churches to discuss Genome Editing becomes now, while developments are still at an early

---

152 McLeish T (2014) *Faith and Wisdom in Science,* OUP.

153 Job 38: 3.

154 Job 38: 4, 8, 22, 24, 25.

155 Job 38: 39.

156 Job 40: 2-4; Job 42: 1-2.

stage. There are important human features which are under single gene control. Mutation in the EPOR Gene which responds to a hormone (The one used by Lance Armstrong) confer exceptional levels of endurance while mutation of the MSTN Genes can lead to greater muscle mass. Are these non-medical interventions a direction in which we want to go? Previous discussions about genetic modification were largely about crops. The new gene editing technologies extend the debate to animals and ourselves. Should we welcome these things, or are there ethical limits to how far we modify our fellow creatures or ourselves?

In humans, gene editing could be used to repair damaged DNA, which could enable treatments for devastating genetic diseases, in adults or children (Somatic Gene Therapy). But the most controversial applications are that it is now possible to alter the genes in an early human embryo. This Germline Gene Therapy results in all the changes being passed on to all future offspring. What is clear is that there are genes such as double muscling which are at the heart of animal breeding for mass and which occur very rarely in humans.[157] Double muscling occurs naturally in breeds such as Belgian Blues, and Piedmontese. These have on average 20% more muscle and a higher meat-to-bone ratio. A single gene, Myostatin, is responsible for normally acting as a break on excess muscle production. Belgian Blues lack 11 DNA letters and Piedmontese have a single letter mutation. In both, the products of the Myostatin gene are defective. This effect is also found in Texel sheep. A boy in Germany has knock-out mutations in both copies of his Myostatin gene. His mother was a professional athlete and heterozygous for the gene. There is interest in using the knowledge to source a treatment for muscle wasting disorders and, of course, for better athletes. Finding such genes and then using them as a base for moving forward seems likely to be an aim in the future.

To be or not to be. Mapping the human genome told us what DNA sequences we had and much about what genes we had, but not all that we needed to know about the functioning of those genes. Genome Editing should make it possible to make changes to genetic sequences which we know are faulty. This offers the prospect of relief from a number of serious genetically linked diseases such as Huntington's. Epigenetics offers a complementary route. Epigenetic modifications to the functioning of

---

157 Doudna J and Sternberg S (2017).

DNA and its associated proteins are characterised by situations of identical genetics but with phenotypic variability and the organism continuing to be impacted by past events. Epigenetics suggests that it may also be possible to make progress by switching off or switching on genes which have been unhelpfully enabled or disabled. The health of the descendants of those who suffered from the Dutch Hunger Winter and parallel situations in some of our major cities, such as Glasgow, would clearly benefit from a reversal of the epigenetic switches which occurred during such a period. Therapies impacting on gene status are being developed.[158] Current drugs impact either histones, DNA methylation or epigenetic enzymes. Enzymes of this type can change one modification at one specific amino acid position on histone proteins. There is hope that such developments may be able to impact transgenerational inheritance. Like Genome Editing of the embryo, such treatments would also have an effect on the unborn by modifying the reprogramming which usually occurs during the production of germ cells and so impacting children and grandchildren.

Overview of the Ethical Issues. It is clear that Genome Editing cannot be given a simple 'yes/no' answer in relation to its acceptability. The case studies reviewed ask if the application is something we should be doing. Unequivocally there are many complex factors. Many of the questions raised by Genome Editing already existed but the ease and breadth of application now make things possible for the first time and set others in a new context.

Looking at human and animal applications together brings out interesting parallels. Existing adults can be consulted and have choice. Animals and embryos do not have choice. We might argue that editing a pig embryo to introduce protection from a serious disease is an expression of animal welfare, humans acting on the pig's behalf. But should parents have their future children modified using Genome Editing in the embryo, to avoid the child having a serious untreatable degenerative disease, or is it wrong to intervene in any human embryo? The embryo cannot speak but will live with the outcome and so will future society.

The birth of the Chinese babies was met with significant but not universal disapproval. It was suggested that there was a moral imperative to aggressively continue pursuing this sort of research because gene editing could eradicate genetic birth deaths and lower the harm of chronic disease.

---

158 Carey N (2012) *The Epigenetics Revolution*, Icon Books, London.

It seems probable that Germline editing will eventually be safe enough to use in clinical situations. Much of the necessary technology is currently in use in IVF clinics. A key question however remains, just because we can edit the human germline does that mean that we should?

The Challenge of being Human. Scripture provides a record of humankind's interaction with God. But the Bible does not give proof texts for 21st century Gene Editing. Rather it lays down the principles and values by which we may make ethical judgements respecting God's laws and principles. Key elements are those associated with our first appearance in the early chapters of Genesis.[159] The great commandment with its focus on love of God and of neighbour helps. The Scriptures explore what it means to be human in relation to our Creator, how we are called to relate to other parts of the creation, and to the various states and conditions of our humanity; for example, we see God's permission to use our fellow creatures, but also the command to care for them.

Healing is a major subject in the New Testament and much of the Gospel accounts are taken up with Jesus' healing activities. Some involved the healing of illnesses which today might be classed as mental or genetically based. On this basis many genetic therapies could be welcomed. They do ask questions.[160] Are disability and suffering unequivocally part of our present human condition? Any reading of Scripture and of history indicate that this has always been so. What is the appropriate balance between eliminating a disability and suffering and devising a strategy for dealing with them? The development of palliative care (Chapter 9) exemplifies an alternative. There are critical illnesses which cannot be 'cured' but the suffering can be alleviated. This is the mission of the hospice movement. There are disabilities which cannot be changed. Christ's compassion provides a model for the healing and caring professions, and motivates a special regard for the disadvantaged. What is unclear is whether the healing which Jesus gave was the removal of the disability or the ability to deal with it.

The suggestion of producing super intelligent humans through embryo screening, even were it possible, would be expensive and would pressurize the current NHS budget. How do we balance expenditure on these new

---

159 Genesis 1: 26-27; Genesis 2: 15-18.
160 Jones DA (2004) *The Soul of the Embryo*, Continuum, London.

technologies with the cost involved in the care of the elderly and of people who no longer have an economic worth? Many of the issues raised in the book highlight issues related to consent, equality and money. Laboratory freezers across the world are full of tissue samples taken without consent. Most would see this as a contribution to the greater good. Some however might object to the uses to which their cells have been put. Companies will make significant sums from the developments which will come from the use of CRISPR.[161] Major companies made large sums of money from Henrietta Lacks' cells.[162] In 2003 Henrietta Lacks son, Sonny, had a quintuple bypass operation. He was told that his mother's cells were one of the most important things that had happened to medicine. Ironically, when he came round from surgery, he was over $100,000 in debt because he couldn't afford to have health insurance! All the developments discussed have issues related to winners and losers and to how benefits are shared across society.

Conclusions

In the beginning the Word already was. The Word was in God's presence and what God was the Word was. He was with God at the beginning and through him all things came to be; without him no created thing came into being. (John 1: 1-3)

This does not give answers, but it does give perspective. Like our readings from Job it causes us to pause and to ask whether we yet know enough to allow us to proceed or whether we need to stop and measure twice before cutting, especially if the change is irreversible. As humans we have invented many things, but we have not created life, and we are yet to understand its complexities. As Job said,

What reply can I give you? I who carry no weight? I know that you can do all things and that no purpose is beyond you.

---

161 Bruce D and Bruce A (1998) 'Patenting Life', pp. 211-244 *in Engineering Genesis: The ethics of genetic engineering in non-human species*, Earthscan Publications Ltd, London.
162 See Chapter 12 for the detail of this.

Chapter 9

End of Life Issues[163]

Thinking by all of us, as individuals, about the nature of our humanity is challenging. We will think of times when we were not here and perhaps, harder, of times when we will not be here. We will consider our role in the totality of humanity.[164] We all tend to see the world as one in which we are, to however a limited extent, a part. However, we know that we have not always existed. Reflecting on non-existence gives a sense of depth to what it means for each of us to be alive and to exist in our own right. This musing leads to thoughts about the world and about 'what it means to be human'.

So, why include a chapter on end of life in a book which is centred on improving life? Previous chapters in this volume have related to issues linked to life and how to enhance it. However, all lives, without exception, eventually come to an end. It has been said *Life is a sexually transmitted degenerative condition with a mortality rate of 100%.*[165] All of us die. Death is not a popular subject for reflection. It's not something we want to think about. We are naturally uncomfortable about contemplating a world where we are no longer a part. As Woody Allen famously said, '*I don't mind dying, I just don't want to be there when it happens.*' However, happen it will and so it's important to consider things which could extend life for some against the need to accept that end of life is an inevitable part of the script.

The prevailing views of the medical profession and of society as a whole do not always prepare us for end of life issues. Against this background Genome Editing can, in some situations, be seen as yet another means

---

163 More detail of some of the science linked to this chapter are to be found in Chapter 12 in the sections on Cohort Studies, He La Cells, Epigenetics and CRISPR.

164 Jones DA (2004) *The Soul of the Embryo*, Continuum, London.

165 Wyatt J (2009) 'A good death, euthanasia and assisted suicide', pp. 191-214, in *Matters of Life and Death*, Intervarsity Press, London.

of postponing an inevitable outcome. In the previous two chapters we have reflected on identity. We suggested that transgenesis could involve a transfer of identity. Genome Editing, to remove what might be classed as a disability, could equally be regarded as making a change in identity and perhaps in an element which relates to mortality. Disability is now viewed differently to how it has been seen in the past. Genome Editing to improve human health will impact on the perception of people who are currently identified as disabled. Many end of life issues link to people with health issues, some with a clear genetic basis, and some where life has become a burden rather than a joy. Covid19 has made this all so much more topical and may have led to a re-ordered perspective. It is for this reason that it seemed helpful to widen the scope of this book and reflect on both end of life and some currently available choices related to this issue. Assisted suicide, sometimes called assisted dying, can be regarded as the ultimate challenge to the 'medical model' and so it is for this reason that it is considered here. Assisted suicide was considered to be such a 'red line' issue that it was selected for discussion by the Anglican Bioethics Group which first met in 2018 under the chairmanship of Brendan McCarthy. Much in this chapter is a product of discussions in that group of which I am also a member.

Before reflecting on assisted suicide there is probably value in asking whether assisted suicide is the same as euthanasia, intentional mercy killing. Both of these were traditionally forbidden. The end point of both is death and with the involvement of someone other than the person who dies. Both are actions and are part of a continuum. A key issue is essentially that of control and decision making. It could be argued that assisted suicide is euthanasia with the consent or even the active encouragement of someone who wishes to die. Euthanasia does not always have this consent. Language is important.[166] A range of terms are used all with related but subtly different overtones e.g. right to die, a merciful death, relief of suffering, assisted dying. The differences can lead to confusion and in an area where it seems important to be clear because the consequences are fatal. The right to die can mean at least 5 different things:

---

166 Wyatt J (2009) *ibid.*

1 The right to say no to life sustaining treatment which seems futile.

2 The right to say no to any life sustaining treatment.

3 The right to commit suicide after rationalized reasoning.

4 The right to get help in committing suicide.

5 The right to be killed by a Doctor at your request.

The literal meaning of 'Euthanasia' is a 'good death.' In the context of our discussion it is perhaps truer to define it as 'the intentional killing, by act or omission, of a person whose life is thought not to be worth living.' This emphasises a number of key elements such as 'intentional', 'act or omission' and 'not worth living' and helps us to see where the similarities and differences are in relation to assisted suicide.

For me the key difference is in terms of who decides that a stage where 'life is not worth living' has been reached. Is it the person who will die, the medical profession or someone else? It's complicated because even when it's the person who will die, as we discuss later in this Chapter, *why* have they reached that decision? It might be fear of pain, of indignity or of dependence. Such fears may or may not be real and may or may not be subject to actions which could minimise them. It is neither simple nor straightforward. It is commonly viewed as being among the ultimate slippery slope issues. It is important to remember in discussion of these issues, but not to overstress, that the 'Charitable Foundation for the Transport of Patients' in 1930's Germany began by organising the transport of mentally disabled people for what seemed, to some, to be good reasons and ended moving millions of Jewish people to their deaths (The Holocaust). All this is why, for so many, assisted suicide is such a major *Red Line*, an issue we return to in discussing the ethical framework within which such decisions lie.[167]

Health and Death

For some, Death is simply the ultimate consequence of ill-health. Health characteristically declines with increasing age. There are of course

---

167   A book which discusses the history of this issue, and comes to a different conclusion from Wyatt, is Parratt J (2020) *So We live, Forever Bidding Farewell*, Sacristy Press, Durham. Parratt considers the issue of 'the slippery slope' in his Chapter 4.

illnesses which affect the very young and sadly some children are born with life threatening illness. Layla Richards (Chapter 5) was one of these. In past times many children died in early life. Many who are currently grandparents or great grandparents will have had siblings or close relatives who died in childhood. The church's tradition of infant baptism is related to this. Fortunately, in the developed world, most children live into adult life.[168] Babies born with a birth weight of 500-700g routinely survive now as do, as a consequence of modern surgery, children born with congenital defects. Nevertheless, there continues to be an association of end of life issues with advancing age.

The impact of ageing. The discussion of issues linked to ageing and the potential role of Science in extending the duration of life have a significant pedigree. In the introduction to this book a Conference held by the Institute of Biology in 1971 was highlighted and comment was made on the number of issues discussed at that time which remain current.[169] Two of its chapters have a particular relevance.[170] Points of continuing relevance include:

- The ageing of machines occurs because frictional forces result in the wearing out of moving parts and the deterioration of key components. That organisms age implies that imperfections appear at a chemical level which cannot be corrected. Imperfections result in deterioration and may be termed ageing.

- Advancing age is usually accompanied by a decline in physical fitness and muscular strength. It is associated with a greater susceptibility to disease and to the effects of accidental damage both of which can result in death. Complex organ systems fail to produce the correct degree of response in relation to environmental forces.

Animals seem to have a life span which is characteristic of the species which suggests a degree of genetic control. The variation in the life span of one-egg twins is less than that of two-egg twins.

---

168 Wyatt J (2009) 'The dying baby, dilemmas of neonatal care', pp. 179-190, *ibid.*

169 Ebling FJ and Heath GW (1972) *The Future of Man*, Academic Press, London.

170 Bellamy D (1972) 'The nature and control of ageing', pp. 113-126, *ibid.* Miller H (1972) 'Keeping people alive', pp. 127-134, *ibid.*

The development of pharmaceuticals has played a major role in preventing premature death from conditions such as pneumonia. A reduction in mortality has resulted in an increase in the proportion of the population living beyond retirement age. Older people represent the fastest growing part of the population This presents important economic and financial problems.

What influences the end of life? The 1946, and subsequent UK Cohort Studies[171] have provided the ability to track a range of people born in the same week, initially in 1946, and to acquire information about them over their lives. This has allowed a better understanding of factors related to health and to death. Among the factors tracked was high blood pressure. The data for the 1946 cohort indicated that many had high blood pressures which could be related to previous factors in life. People born into a lower social class tended to have a higher blood pressure as adults. High blood pressure was associated with being overweight.

Both of these could be related to the start of life factors. Babies with a low birth weight tended to have higher blood pressure as adults. This linked to findings in a study known as the UK Death Atlas[172] which related cause of death to living in different areas of the country. Deaths from heart disease between 1968 and 1978 were higher in parts of Wales and the North of England and was correlated with infant mortality between 1921 and 1925. Poor nutrition before and immediately after birth killed many and left many of the survivors more susceptible to heart disease decades later.

This of course parallels the well documented effects of the Dutch Hunger Winter which was noted in relation to epigenetic effects (Chapters 7 and 12). Epigenetics clearly impacts length of life. This information and the findings related to it have been controversial because it challenges the view that chronic disease is a function of a poor adult life-style. Could Genome Editing be seen as a way of reducing the worrying concept of determinism? Does Genome Editing represent further options for avoiding things which might have been seen as inevitable, meant to be?

---

171 Pearson H (2016) *The Life Project*, Allen Lane, London.
172 Gardner MJ *et al* (1984) *Atlas of mortality from selected diseases in England and Wales 1968-1978.*

So, what is death? In Chapters 8 and 12 mention is made of the American woman Henrietta Lacks who died in 1951. Tumour cells taken from her before her death, now known as HeLa cells, are still alive and multiplying today.[173] This gives an interesting starting point for a reflection on death and immortality. Henrietta Lacks was born on the 18th of August 1920. Hospital records show that she died on 4th October 1951. However, her cells live on. One hundred years on she, her cells at least, don't make her the oldest person alive or that has ever lived, but the range of uses to which her cells are being put suggest that there will come a day when she will be the 'oldest person ever'. In her life Henrietta was a daughter a sister, a wife, a mother. She lived and died without being noticed by many outwith her immediate family. The coincidence of her being ill in a hospital in Baltimore, the hospital having scientists interested in cell culture, and diseases needing cultured cells, came together to make her immortal and allowed her to save the lives of many including all of those who did not contract Polio, and to impact the lives of even more.

Psalm 103 says:

> *The days of a mortal are as grass; he blossoms like a wild flower in the meadow: a wind passes over him, and he is gone, and his place knows him no more. But the Lord's love is for ever on those who fear him.* (Psalm 103: 15-17a)

While on Retreat, prior to Ordination, in a Redemptorist Monastery near Perth, I was given this part of the Psalms as a passage for reflection and later discussion. It is a profound piece which is not uncommonly used at funerals but I objected to the words '*he is gone, and his place knows him no more*'. As a biologist who has worked on plant root systems and their associated micro-organisms, I was aware that when a plant dies and when its roots die, they leave a micro-biological and physical imprint in the soil. The microbiology of the area around the dead root is different to that of bulk soil. The roots of different species leave behind different microbial footprints.

In addition, after its death the root leaves a biopore, a space in the soil which has been stabilised as a result of its decomposition. If this is

---

173 Skloot R (2010) *The Immortal Life of Henrietta Lacks*, Macmillan, London.

true for a plant root surely it is also true for humans. Writers, artists, recording artists, film stars all leave a legacy which continues after them. Parents leave a genetic legacy in their offspring and their offspring's children. Friends leave a legacy in our memories. How do we and might we leave a legacy?

This is considered to be equally true in spiritual terms.[174] Prior to 1914 there was fear of divine judgement. The concept of purgatory had been devised. The magnitude of losses in the Great War forced a change in how the church came to view such issues. After the first World War the Bishop of London assured the country:

> Those dear young men, they are not dead. They were never more alive than five minutes after death. They love still those they have loved on earth and they live a fuller life than this.

This change in view of what happened beyond death was linked in time to an increasing emphasis on the importance of the current life, the need to change social and political conditions with 'the hope for life after death' becoming a distraction from the most urgent task for humans. These have a significant impact on how we regard the end of life. All of this is well summarised by the medic Atul Gawande who commented:

> Being mortal involves a struggle with the limits set by our genes and the resulting cells, flesh and bones. Medicine has aided us in expanding some of these limits, but this power is finite. Medicine all too easily can become focused on health and survival, but it ought to be wider than that and be aware of the importance of well-being, a key reason for being alive. This is a reason at the end of life but also during life's journey. Such a view would mean that when an injury or illness occurs it becomes important to ask about hopes and fears and perhaps most of all the trade offs that each person is willing to make. This would then set the role of the caring professions as helping people within the limits the individual has prescribed. Interventions must relate to such aims. [175]

---

174 Harries R (1995) 'Attitudes to death in the twentieth century', pp. 32-46 *in Questioning Belief*, SPCK, London.

175 Gawande A (2015) *Being Mortal*, Profile Books, London.

Thus, it would be easy to think of modern medical techniques as being primarily a means of staving off the end of life. In a recent book Richard Holloway reflects on end of life issues.[176] Reflecting on the medical professions he suggested:

- We spend most of our lives not thinking about death which perhaps is just as well as we may not have much control over the last part of our lives.

- Death and the dying process leading to it have been taken over by the medical profession who all too often see death as an enemy who must be fought and death as a battle lost.

- The inevitability of death suggests the need to see it as being the fall of a curtain at the conclusion of our role in the play which is our lives.

He went on to conclude anguish is part of being human. However maybe it's time in the world as it is today that, instead of chasing that elusive 'ideal' image, we learn to be happy in our skin, enjoy what we have, grow old gracefully and accept we all die sometime.

A Reflection on Life. A Christian contribution to ethical debates within society may be unapologetically Christian, but will rarely be exclusively Christian. While key theological beliefs form the foundation on which the Church develops its guiding ethical principles and practices, it's important that they be considered on their merits and not just as unquestionable elements of faith. Similar ethical principles and practices can emerge from a variety sources, including some which are unambiguously secular. In an inclusive society faith ought to be accepted as providing as valid a foundation as alternative philosophies, but many of these seek to replace a faith led approach with an approach of their own. A healthy society needs to be pluralistic, especially in relation to end of life issues, and recognise that many of the Church's beliefs are widely shared. Clarifying core beliefs is an important step to debating key areas such as end of life issues including assisted suicide.[177]

---

176 Holloway R (2018) *Waiting for the Last Bus*, Canongate Books, Edinburgh.

177 Derived from a Reflection, 'A Christian basis for engaging in public debates on medical ethics', written by Dr Rory Corbett for the Anglican Bioethics Group.

Continuing the Story. There are illnesses which are incurable. Some of these can result in the sufferer having a poor quality of life and being unable to do anything for themselves. This puts a number of questions to us, and the answers take us into controversial areas. Are there times when we need to accept that life has become a burden and that improvement is improbable? In such situations should people be able to *ask for help* to die? Suicide in any event and 'assisting suicide' for many in society are a 'red line' issue and so just somewhere where we ought not to go.

This is one of the ultimate ethical questions which can only be answered 'Yes' or 'No'. Answering 'No', and concluding that it should not be allowable, because it would mean crossing an important red line in society, ends all discussion.

The current legal position on assisted suicide is founded on the importance of this red line. (It is only relatively recently that unassisted suicide has been decriminalised in parts of the UK.) If the answer to the question 'should I be able to *ask for help* to die' is 'Yes', then assisted suicide would not *always* cross the red line, and so discussion continues and a number of consequential questions arise. These include, would permitting assisted suicide be too open to exploitation? What should we do to minimise this? Who might be allowed to assist?

Although the primary interest in this topic lies in ethical issues and issues which impinge on Christian faith, it can help to look at the current legal position on assisted suicide as a guide to the mind of society. Parliament makes laws and the Courts interpret them. Together these are meant to represent the public mind. Whether assisted suicide ought to be permitted in UK remains a live issue and is a distinctive element of 'what it means to be human'. The expressed minds of law makers and law interpreters help to demonstrate the practical complexity and the ambivalence of the public mind.

Case Studies

Assisted suicide has recently been the subject of a number of Appeals to the UK Supreme Court. These cases and their associated judgements set out the issues involved, and The case studies here are drawn from recent appellants to that court.[178]

Tony suffered a catastrophic stroke when he was aged 51. As a result, he was completely paralysed, save that he could move his head and his eyes. He was able to communicate, but only laboriously, by blinking to spell out words, letter by letter, initially via a Perspex board, and subsequently via an eye blink computer. Despite loving and devoted attention from his family and carers he had consistently regarded his life as 'dull, miserable, demeaning, undignified and intolerable', and had wished to end it.

Because of his paralysed state, Tony was unable to fulfil his wish of ending his life without assistance, other than by self-starvation, a potentially protracted exercise, involving considerable pain and distress. His preference was for someone to kill him by injecting him with a lethal drug, such as a barbiturate, but if that was not acceptable, he was prepared to kill himself by means of a machine which, after being loaded with a lethal drug, could be set up so as to be digitally activated by Tony, using a pass phrase, via an eye blink computer. He was told that it would be unlawful for someone to kill him or assist him in killing himself. Tony embarked on the very difficult and painful course of self-starvation, refusing all nutrition, fluids, and medical treatment, and died of pneumonia on 22 August 2012.

Martin suffered a brainstem stroke in August 2008, when he was 43. He is almost completely unable to move and can only communicate thorough slow hand movements and via an eye blink computer. His condition is incurable, and, despite being devotedly looked after by his wife and carers, he wishes to end his life, which he regards as undignified, distressing and intolerable, as soon as possible. Apart from self-starvation, Martin's only way of achieving this is by travelling to Zurich in Switzerland to make use of the Dignitas service, which, lawfully under Swiss law, enables people who wish to die to do so. However, he first needs:

---

178 The Supreme Court (2014) Press Summary R (on the application of Nicklinson and another) appellants v Ministry of justice (Respondent) R (on the application of AM) (AP) (Respondent) The Director of Public Prosecution (Appellant) [2014] UKSC 38 on appeal from [2013] EWCA Civ 961.

to find out about this service,

to join Dignitas,

to obtain his medical records,

to send money to Dignitas, and

to have someone accompany him to Zurich.

These are tragic stories. They were all part of an Appeal to the UK Supreme Court. Much of what follows is taken from the judgement of that court.

Issues raised. Legal cases related to Assisted Suicide, have been common over the last 20 years. It is an issue currently being discussed by the UK Anglican Bioethics group. The discussions within that group have impacted much of what is written here. Over a decade ago the Director of Public Prosecutions (DPP) was required by the Courts to provide guidance on how decisions to prosecute cases of assisting a suicide would be taken. Over the period from 2009 to 2019 there were 152 referrals to the police with 3 resulting in a successful prosecution. Definitive guidance on the subject comes from the following:[179]

1) The DPP's guidance, produced first in 2010 and updated in 2014. (Suicide: policy for Prosecutors in respect of cases of encouraging or assisting suicide).[180]

2) The Judgement of the Supreme Court on the Cases where the judgement was given in 2014.[181]

Text from these cases helps to set out both the current legal situation and the logic involved in the decision-making process. The cases cover two particular situations:

Where people who are suffering from terminal illnesses and wish to end their lives but are physically unable to do so and so would need assistance to commit suicide, and

Where someone who is suffering from a terminal illness is currently able to commit suicide but wants to leave the act until the point when their quality of life becomes unsatisfactory when they would need assistance.

---

179 Material on this is available from the UK Supreme Court's web site.

180 Director of Public Prosecutions (2014) Suicide Policy for Prosecutors in Respect of Cases of Encouraging or Assisting Suicide CPS, GOV.UK.

181 The Supreme Court (2014) *ibid.*

The President of the Supreme Court, Lord Neuberger, set out the Key considerations in the following terms.

> The vulnerability to pressure of the old or terminally ill is a formidable problem. The problem is not that people may decide to kill themselves who are not fully competent mentally. I am prepared to accept that mental competence is capable of objective assessment by health professionals. The real difficulty is that even the mentally competent may have reasons for deciding to kill themselves, which reflect either overt pressure upon them by others or their own assumptions about what others may think or expect. The difficulty is particularly acute in the case of 'indirect social pressure'.

The low self-esteem many old or severely ill and dependent people have of themselves i.e. their perceived identity, combined with the negative perceptions of most patients about the views of those around them is at the heart of the matter. Most contemplating suicide for health-related reasons will be aware of their dependence on others. Disabilities may arise from illness, injury, or old age. A perception of being a burden may be the result of overt pressure, but may arise from patients placing a low value on their own lives and assuming that others do too.

Feelings of uselessness are likely to be particularly acute in those who were highly active. The contrast between now and then can be particularly painful. A concern is that the legalisation of assisted suicide would be followed by its progressive normalisation- a world where suicide was regarded as just another optional end-of-life choice.

The President of the Supreme Court summed up its thoughts on this matter in the following terms.

> It is one thing to assess someone's mental ability to form a judgment, but another to discover their true reasons for a decision and to assess the quality of the reasons. I doubt whether it is possible in most cases to distinguish between those who have spontaneously formed the desire to kill themselves and those who have done so in response to real or imagined pressures. There is a good deal of evidence that this problem exists, that it is significant, and that it is aggravated by negative modern attitudes to old age and sickness-related disability.

Samson. What can we learn from Scripture? What we can learn from the Biblical character Samson? Samson was one of the Judges who 'ruled' Israel before it had its first King. He was a great military leader. Following an unfortunate liaison with Delilah he was captured and blinded by the Philistines. His death is described in the following terms:

> *They stood him between the pillars and Samson said to the boy who led him by the hand 'put me where I can feel the pillars which support the temple' so that I may lean against them. Samson called to the Lord and said remember me for this one occasion God give me strength and let me at one stroke be avenged on the Philistines for my two eyes. He put his arms around the two central pillars which supported the temple and bracing himself said let me die with the Philistines Then Samson leaned forward with all his might and the Temple crashed down.'* (Judges 16: 25-30)

For Samson life had become impossible. He wanted to die. He wanted his death to have meaning and to be a fitting end to all he had achieved in life. He needed help to bring about his death and for it to be the ending he wanted for his life. Were the actions of the boy a parallel to assisting a suicide? All of this seems to speak into many secular situations. What can a secular world learn from people of faith?

Challenges to Being Human

Christians are not distinct from the wider population in relation to these challenges. In his novel *Barchester Towers* Anthony Trollope begins with the conflicting thoughts of one of the central characters in the book, Archdeacon Grantly, at the time of the impending death of his father, Bishop Grantly. If Bishop Grantly died quickly then the Archdeacon would become Bishop but, because the Government was about to fall, if the Bishop did not die quickly, he would not. We read:

> The illness of the good old man was long and lingering and became at last a matter of intense interest to those concerned whether the new appointment should be made by a Conservative or Liberal government. Bishop Grantly died as he had lived, peaceably, slowly, without pain and without excitement. The breath ebbed from him almost imperceptibly, and for a month before his death it was a question as to whether he was

alive or dead. The Bishop was on his last legs; but the ministry was also tottering. Dr Grantly tried to keep his mind away from the subject but he could not. The race was so very close. He looked at the dying man's impassive placid face. Now he laid sleeping like a baby, resting easily on his back, his mouth just open; his breath was perfectly noiseless and his thin wan hand, which lay above the coverlet never moved. Nothing could be easier than the old man's passage from this world to the next.

But by no means easy were the emotions of him who sat there watching. He knew it must be now or never. No probable British Prime Minister but he who was now in, he who was soon to be out, would think of making a Bishop of Dr Grantly. Thus, he thought long and sadly in deep silence, and then gazed at that still living face, and then at last dared to ask himself whether he really longed for his father's death. The effort was a salutary one, and the question was answered in a moment. 'God bless you my dears,' said the Bishop with feeble voice as he woke; and so, he died. The Archdeacon's mind however had already travelled from the death Chamber to the closet of the Prime Minister. He had brought himself to pray for his father's life but now that that life was done, minutes were too precious to be lost – useless to lose everything for the pretence of a foolish sentiment. How was he to forget his father the Bishop – to overlook what he had lost and think only of what he might possibly gain?

This identifies conflicted thoughts we may have around the death of someone close to us. It indicates that there are ever mixed emotions. If this is the case in respect of anticipated natural deaths, then it must be harder in relation to facilitating the passage of someone close to us. The Christian doctor and ethicist John Wyatt suggested that however compassionate are our motives involvement in the killing of someone else will always impact our humanity.[182]

What is more, most Christians would not collude with arguments about being 'a burden on others' or the perception of being 'a useless person'. Also, most would not accept claims to 'unbridled personal autonomy'. For most people nearing the end of their life certain needs dominate conscious and

182 Wyatt J (2009) 'A good death? Euthanasia and assisted Suicide', pp. 191-214, *ibid*.

unconscious thoughts.[183] How we value ourselves. In our society, 'value' is frequently measured in terms of productivity, occupation, wealth, looks etc. So, did my life really matter? What is my identity? Am I still valued by my family and society?[184]

Such thoughts are unavoidable. Most of us have them during normal life from time to time. As end of life issues, they become just that much more prevalent. This suggests that to legalise the concept that there are lives which are not worth living could have potentially serious consequences. The terminally ill and those suffering great pain from incurable illnesses are often vulnerable. Not all families with interests at stake are wholly unselfish and loving. There is a risk that assisted suicide may be abused in the sense that people may be persuaded that they want to die or that they ought to want to die.

This leads to questions around confidence. Does a worthwhile future remain, essentially is there still hope? Death threatens all relationships. People of faith need to be clear that they are loved by God and that if there have been rifts in this relationship that they will be overcome. Reconciliation with one's self, others and God matters.

These needs suggest a Christian response to those approaching the end of life. Every human life has value because all are created in the image of God. Humanity is not a consumer product. This is an issue revisited (Chapter 3) within the responses to the Corona virus where it is now clear that Government and some in the NHS did regard some lives as being of less value than others. Christians believe in interdependence and reject the notion of us being wholly in control. Dignity lies in our identity as children of the God who has made us and who loves us. All of this returns us to how we view suffering and disability. Jesus died in excruciating pain, but his dignity remained intact.

Another important issue is how we view and interpret compassion. Those who want to change the law have compassionate motives – but they

---

183 I am grateful to the UK Anglican Bioethics group for these thoughts and in particular to James Newcombe, Bishop of Carlisle, who developed them in an address on the subject.

184 Miller H (1972) 'Keeping people alive', pp. 127-134 in Ebling FJ and Heath GW (1971) *The Future of Man*, Academic Press, London.

have no monopoly on compassion. Palliative care, an alternative to suicide, is also about compassion and it's about seeing a patient as still a person and responding accordingly.

The current legal position. The current system of guidance is detailed in the following terms:[185]

> The policy of the DPP is to investigate any assisted suicide after the event, and to lean against prosecuting where the assister was a close relative or friend activated by compassion. Furthermore, it is clear that those people who, out of compassion, assist relations and friends who wish to commit suicide, by taking or accompanying them to Dignitas, are routinely not prosecuted. In other words, those people who have access to supportive friends and relations, and who possess the means and physical ability to travel to Switzerland, are able in practice to be assisted in their wish to commit suicide, whereas those people who lack one or more of those advantages, cannot receive such assistance.

The DPP issued a draft policy, identifying factors, which would favour Prosecution, and others which would point against Prosecution. These are interesting in the context of the relationship between the Law and public perceptions. The legal response is likely to be dominated by the clarity of the evidence in each case alongside the accepted motive of the person assisting the suicide.

Conclusions

The ethical issues in the assisted Dying debate were set out by the President of the Supreme Court in the following terms:

> The subject of euthanasia and assisted dying have been deeply controversial 'for a very long time': The arguments and counter arguments have ranged widely. There is a conviction that human life is sacred and that the corollary is that euthanasia and assisted suicide are always wrong. The Roman Catholic Church, Islam and other religions support this view. There is also a secular view, shared sometimes by atheists and agnostics, that human life is sacred.

---

185 Director of Public Prosecutions (2014) Suicide Policy for Prosecutors in Respect of Cases of Encouraging or Assisting Suicide CPS, GOV.UK.

In contrast there are of course millions who do not hold these beliefs. For many the personal autonomy of individuals is predominant. They would argue that it is the moral right of individuals to have a say over the time and manner of their death. However, we live as part of society and so there is a shared responsibility. To the question of 'who is my neighbour?', we have clear spiritual guidance.[186] This has resonance with end of life situations.[187]

It is also argued that euthanasia and assisted suicide, under medical supervision, would undermine the trust between doctors and patients. It is said that protective safeguards are unworkable. Think Harold Shipman, Ian Paterson, The East Kent Health Trust etc.

The physician Atul Gawande[188] commented that when training for a career in medicine the clear purpose was to save lives not to tend to their demise. Medicine struggles to easily come to terms with an acceptance of death as a solution. This has ever presented a problem for the NHS. It is commonly suggested that the NHS is now the National Religion of the UK, the key thing which links, unifies and sets the beliefs of the nation. Given the NHS's emphasis on treating illness and keeping people alive, coming to terms with end of life is always going to be difficult. A vision of the curtain coming down because life had reached that point in the script but that there was more of a different kind to come, does not sit easily in current society.

In the Covid19 outbreak some of the above assumed priorities changed (as detailed in Chapter 3). The risk of death in younger patients seemed to shape priorities *within the NHS*. It has also led to urgent consideration and much new thinking about the relationship between the quality of life and prolonged life. This is part of the natural order of things. It raises the question when should we fix things and when should we leave alone? Again, I'm tempted to add 'Discuss'. The countervailing contentions of moral philosophers, medical experts and ordinary people are endless. The literature is vast. But it is of great importance to note that these are ancient questions on which millions in the past have taken diametrically opposite views and still do.

---

186 Luke 10: 25-37.
187 Genesis 2: 15-17. See also Miller H (1972) 'Keeping People Alive', pp. 127-133 in *The Future of Man*; Messer N (2002) 'Death', pp. 125-127 in *Theological Issues in Bioethics*, ed. N Messer, Darton, Longman and Todd, London.
188 Gawande A (2014) *Being Mortal*, Profile Books, London.

Does Scripture help? How does Samson help us? He was a man who decided that killing himself was the way out. Yes, in doing so he killed many of his captors but in killing them he killed himself. A passage from the New Testament seems helpful:

> *Jesus then came with his disciples to a place called Gethsemane and he said to them sit here while I go over there to pray. Distress and Anguish overwhelmed him He said to them my heart is ready to break with grief. Stop here and stay awake with me. Then he went a little further, threw himself down and prayed My father if it is possible let this cup pass me by. Yet not my will but yours. Then he came to the disciples and said to them still asleep? Still resting? The hour has come The Son of Man is betrayed.* (Matthew 26: 36-46)

This passage from the Gospel of Matthew puts things into context. Jesus gave up his life because it was what had been ordained. He clearly did not want to. The crucifixion led to the Resurrection and to all that we are promised. Why was that sacrifice needed? Why was that sacrifice needed for humanity? These are truly key issues for reflection.

Chapter 10

The Reality of Now: Climate Change

Why include a chapter on Climate Change in a book which is predominantly about the impact of developments in biology? Before the advent of Covid19, Climate Change dominated the news. Even in the midst of a Covid19 pandemic the effects of Climate Change continue and the need for mitigation has not become any less important than it was at the beginning of 2020. Climate change will be with us as a major issue for long after Covid19 has ceased to be the predominant issue it is currently. Climate Change can be defined in biological terms as resulting from an inability of current living organisms, including humanity, to match the quantities of carbon they release and store, to that stored by earlier generations of living beings. Even in these terms it's clear that the out-workings of biology interact with societal forces. This could establish a biological base for Climate Change, but the remit of this book is beyond mere biology. My remit as illustrated in the chapters on 'end of life' (Chapter 9) and' sexuality' (Chapter 7) is to explore our humanity by getting beneath the biology to reflect upon what our reaction to such issues tells us about 'what it means to be human'. This is important to both identifying the future role of Genome Editing and to a continuing journey with Scripture informed by such developments. Context and key issues concerning society are vital. Climate Change is an issue shaping society and will be a factor influencing the extent to which the issues of this book become practical concerns.[189]

Beginning this story

In 1993 a conference was held on the subject of Global Climate Change.[190] The predictions made at that time of the likely impact closely

189 Bradley I (1990) *God is Green*, Darton, Longman and Todd, London.
190 Atkinson D (1993) *Global Climate Change*, BCPC Monograph no 56, BCPC, Farnham, Surrey.

resemble current views. However, then, it was felt that yes, Climate Change would be major, just not quite yet. That being the case we had time to analyse, to plan mitigation and to adjust. It is interesting to look back and to ask did we use that time wisely? In reviewing the impact of Climate Change[191] three major driving forces were identified:

- Atmospheric Composition Change
- Change in Climate
- Change in Land Use

It was suggested that most had become accustomed to a world which was essentially stable. There had been little Ice Ages in the recent past, and major Ice Ages over 100,000 years ago but we had become used to a climate which generally was dependable. The current crisis is based on finding that this reliance was no longer dependable. Human actions had been altering the composition of the atmosphere resulting in more incoming radiant energy being trapped within the atmosphere and resulting in an alteration to the climate. That human action *can* alter fundamental global processes is a radical and different notion. It has been contested, especially by those with vested interests in maintaining the current norm. There are significant numbers of Climate Change deniers.

Climate Change results from the generation of greenhouse gases (principally CO^2) as a result of human activities, gases which are subsequently released into the atmosphere. Over the history of our planet the release of such gasses through natural processes, the 'greenhouse' effect, has been keeping the earth warm and thus habitable for millennia. The additional concentrations of 'greenhouse' gases resulting from human activity are making the greenhouse too hot and as a result less stable. The use of fossil fuels such as coal and oil, reinject into the atmosphere CO^2 fixed at a much earlier time. A balance sheet for CO^2 shows that of the 8.5 Gt per year released, 6 Gt come from fossil fuels with around half staying in the atmosphere and causing the 'heating problem'. The concentration of CO^2 in the atmosphere has increased from 280ppm in the pre-industrial

---

191 Tinker PB (1993) 'Climate Change and its Implications', pp. 3-12, *ibid*.

era to a figure close to 380 ppm. This has been associated with an average global temperature rise of around 1.5 degrees. In addition to industrial and domestic causes, factors related to land use are also an important element. However commonly, many emissions are balanced by fixation by forests, grassland and crops.

Other key gases are methane and nitrous oxide. All three major greenhouse gases are intimately bound up with agriculture and food production. Methane is released from the decomposition of animal wastes and from the ruminant process in cattle and sheep. Nitrous oxide is generated from soil processes. It is important to remember that while agricultural and forestry processes emit greenhouse gases they also fix and store Carbon and so unlike all other human activities they sit on both sides of the balance sheet.

Land use change is complex. Although influenced by Climate Change it is also a product of commercial forces. The pressure to produce food is different in the developed and in the developing world (Chapters 4&6). These pressures impact on the ability to reforest or the pressure to deforest.

More rapid fluctuations in climate,[192] changes to maximum and minimum temperatures, the seasons and the intensity and patterns of rainfall will impact our ability to secure the food supply which is part of our current normal. Temperature will increase in general but with huge spatial variation. Rainfall will also increase but often with reductions in the summer period. The past decade has shown the impact of both variation and of extremes. The news on 23rd August 2020 recorded both forest fires in California as a result of blistering heat, and snow in Australia as a result of unusual movement of cold air from the Antarctic. Changes such as these are likely to impact on World food supply.[193] Changes in food supply are likely to depend on two distinct components (also discussed in Chapters 4&6):

---

192   Rowntree PR (1993) 'Climatic Models: Changes in Physical Environmental Conditions', pp. 13-32 in *Global Climate Change*.

193   Parry M and Rosenzweig C (1993) 'The Potential Effects of Climate Change on World Food Supply', pp. 33-55, *ibid*.

1 Changes in Crop Yields. These will vary from region to region and from crop to crop. Maize seems likely to be adversely affected and soya much less so. Adverse effects are due to a potential reduction in the length of the growing season and to reduced water availability during crop growth.

2 The Response of the World Food Trade. This will depend on the extent of trade liberalisation, rates of economic growth and population growth. The ability of the trade system to absorb the impact falls with the size of the impact. Developed countries are expected to be less severely impacted. Population growth is among the factors having the greatest potential impact.

All of this will also have consequences on how our food is produced and the role of genetics in either increasing or in sustaining production. This matters as much for organic production[194] as for what is promoted as genetically enhanced production.[195]

Case study

The Falkland Estate. For over a decade I was involved in the farming of The Falkland Estate in Fife, Scotland, at a time when it was considering its environmental footprint and response to Climate Change. This responsibility over-lapped with my role in the development of the Scottish Government's Food Strategy[196] as Chair of a working group on access, security and affordability[197] which included consideration of the contribution of food production, distribution and consumption to Climate Change.

Agriculture in Scotland faces two major restrictions, climate and soils.

194 Ronald PC and Adamchak RW (2008) *Tomorrows Table: Organic farming, genetics and the future of food*, OUP.
195 Avise JC (2004) *The Hope, Hype and Reality of Genetic Engineering*, OUP.
196 Recipe for Success – Scotland's National Food and Drink Policy, Scottish Government, Edinburgh (2009). Leadership Forum Report: Development of the National Food and Drink Policy, Scottish Government, Edinburgh (2009).
197 Anon (2009) The Implications for Scotland of Food Affordability, Access and Security, Scottish Government, Edinburgh.

Scotland receives a lower intensity of radiation (Sunlight) and less total radiation than more southerly parts of the UK and much of continental Europe. This means that temperatures, particularly soil temperatures in the Spring, are lower and the risk of frosts continues until later in the year. This limits the range of crops which can be grown and increases the risks of poor yields. This impacts particularly on crops which need a long growing season (e.g. many fruits) It has less adverse consequences on wholly vegetative crops such as grass. The history of glaciation in Scotland has left Scotland with varied soils. This limits farm size because of the increase in management input necessary to run a farm with many different types of soil. It has resulted in shallow soils which also limit production.

Soils and climate limit production at Falkland. Limited cereal production is possible but most of the land is best used to grow grass to be grazed by cattle or sheep. As part of making production sustainable the Estate adopted Organic Standards. This recognised that while the production of food is important it is not the only issue – there are[198] issues linked to culture and social interactions in relation to a historic estate. Ultimately the real issues are beyond whether a type of agriculture produces 9 or 10 tonnes per hectare of wheat.[199] Going organic means reduced inputs of fertilisers and pesticides, whose production uses fossil fuels and whose use can accentuate the release of nitrous oxide from soil. It is also beneficial for wild life, and makes optimum use of soils of limited quality and the nutrients mobilised by the different crops in the rotation. Although focusing much of production on ruminant animals – which produce methane as part of their digestive process and would increase the greenhouse gas profile – because stock was being grass fed, this would minimise, but not eliminate, the methane release. In addition, grazed grassland is a substantial fixer of atmospheric carbon and so promotes long term soil carbon storage.

The organic decision linked to two concepts which are important to

---

198 Atkinson D and Watson CA (2020) Science and organic agriculture, pp. 1-23 in The Science beneath Organic Production, Wiley London.
199 Atkinson D and Watson CA (2020) The science beneath organic production Wiley, London.

Climate Change:

- Co-existence
- Inherent value

Organic agriculture like all farming is a business which aims to produce food. This overall approach is the predominant means of food production across the globe. Most of the world's population are fed with food which could meet organic standards. The underpinning ethos of different types of food production are discussed in Chapter 4.[200] Co-existence with nature, involving people and getting a balance needs continuing management input, but ultimately may be more sustainable.

We live in a society aware of value for money. Reducing the price of food to consumers has been a stated aspiration. Supermarkets compete predominantly on the basis of price. Quality, especially appearance, is a consideration but focuses on what can be measured. Organic production aims to impact quality both in measurable ways but also in ways described as 'inherent'.[201] The 'inherent' concept describes production which is fair to the environment and to producers, resulting in food with qualities which may not be measurable but are never the less real.

Noah and Joseph. Climate Change is complex so two biblical figures have been selected to address the issues involved. Changes in rainfall patterns, especially in the winter months and over the last decade bring Noah to mind. Issues related to feeding a hungry world if reduced food supply results from Climate Change suggests that Joseph might also help the reflections.

Noah 'was a righteous man'.[202] God had decided to bring the human race to an end because it had become corrupt. He instructed Noah to make an ark because the earth was about to be flooded. Noah was allowed to save his family and was instructed to bring into the ark every kind of bird, beast and creeping thing. It then rained for 40 days and flooded the earth killing everything not in the ark. The ark floated above the waters which

200 Atkinson D and Walker R (2020) Crop protection and food quality, pp. 213-236 in the Science beneath organic production, Wiley, London.
201 Atkinson D et al (2012) Food Security: The approach of the Scottish churches. Rural Theology, 10. 27-42.
202 Genesis 6: 9.

even covered the mountains. After 150 days the water began to subside. Noah sent out a dove to see if the flood had yet ended. We read:

The dove found no place where she could settle because all the earth was under the water and so she came back to him and to the ark. He waited seven more days and again sent out the dove from the ark. She came back to him towards evening with a freshly plucked olive leaf in her beak. Noah knew then that the water had subsided from the earth's surface. He waited another seven days and when he sent out the dove, she did not come back to him. So, Noah removed the hatch and looked out and he saw that the ground was dry. (Genesis 8: 9-13)

We then get God's reaction and a new covenant with man and animals.

God spoke to Noah. Come out of the ark, bring out every living creature that is with you and let them spread over the earth and be fruitful and increase on it. The Lord said never again shall I put the earth under a curse because of mankind however their inclinations may be nor shall I ever again kill all living creatures. (Genesis 8: 21)

Climate Change is a global phenomenon. It affects all of us. Noah reminds us that actions can have significant consequences and that while humans are important to God so are other parts of the creation. Our actions threaten more than ourselves.

Joseph. The story is long, taking up 14 of the 50 chapters of Genesis. It establishes why and how the people of Israel were in Egypt and so leads us into the context of Exodus. The key issue here are the issues around famine. A complex story resulted in Joseph ending up in Egypt and as the principle servant of Pharaoh. This resulted from his ability to interpret dreams and in particular Pharaoh's dreams of good and thin cows and ears of grain. Joseph saw that seven years of good production would be followed by seven years of famine. He counselled:

Pharaoh should take one fifth of the produce of Egypt during the seven years of plenty. All the food produced in the good years should be put under control as a store of food against the seven years of famine. This will be a reserve of food. (Genesis 41: 34-36)

Joseph was given the job of organising all of this:

Joseph gathered all the food produced in Egypt then and stored it in the towns putting in each the food from the surrounding country He stored the grain in huge quantities. (Genesis 41: 48-49)

After the period of plenty there was, as he had predicted, famine:

There was famine in every country . . . When the whole land was in the grip of famine, Joseph opened all the granaries and sold grain to the Egyptians, for the famine was severe. The whole world came to Egypt to buy grain from Joseph, so severe was the famine everywhere. (Genesis 41: 54, 56-7)

Joseph is remembered for the relief of famine, but:

There was no food anywhere, so very severe was the famine . . . Joseph gathered in all the money in Egypt and in Canaan in exchange for the grain which the people bought, and put it in Pharaoh's treasury. When the money in Egypt and Canaan had come to an end, the Egyptians all came to Joseph, "Give us food," they said . . . Joseph replied, "If your money is all gone, hand over your livestock, and I shall give you food in return." . . . The year came to an end, and in the following year they came to him and said, ". . . There is nothing left for your lordship but our bodies and our lands. Take us and our land in payment for food . . . Give us seed-corn to keep us alive, or we shall die and our land will become desert." So Joseph acquired for Pharaoh all the land in Egypt. (Genesis 47: 13-20)

Joseph averted starvation, but as a result the people lost stock, land and independence. Food came at a price. Climate Change will impact these factors. Major pandemics such as Covid19 may have similar impact.

New Questions

Life depends on assumptions. We unconsciously assume much about our world. We assume that there will be seasons and they will have predictable characteristics. It will be cold in winter in the Northern hemisphere so we need warm clothes and an ability to heat our homes. We assume summer will be much warmer so we will spend more time out of doors. We assume that there will be rain so crops will grow and we will have water to drink. Essentially, we assume the physical environment will be predictable so we can plan. It was one thing we didn't need to worry about. Then came Climate Change. The increased onset of winter floods, disturbed seasonal patterns, rising summer temperatures all reinforced awareness that climate was changing and that it was no longer reliable. In addition, we became clear that this was as a result of how we lived. We were responsible. Change would continue unless we altered our lifestyles. These changes also impacted other living things. Our actions were leading to species extinction. This raised one big question: What did we intend to do about it? There were subsidiary questions: What can I as an individual do? What ought my country to do? What is the role of Government? How do we work together across the globe? Is there a balance to be struck between countries at different stages of 'development'? How do we develop a strategy which is optimum for both humans and for other living things?

What do we need to understand? Modelling Climate Change has shown the limits to our level of understanding.[203] Modelling is crucial to both Climate Change and to the management of Covid19. In both of these areas the individual models used, their predictions and the actions following the predictions have been controversial. So, what is modelling? Modelling involves the production of descriptions of a system or of an event using a set of variables and equations that establish relationships i.e. they produce mathematical simulations based on the best current information. Climate Change models, especially general circulation models, tend to be based on what we know of air circulation and energy balances. Covid19 models, such as those developed by Neil Ferguson's team at Imperial College London, depend on epidemiological data. They are thus precise statements, in mathematical terms, of best estimates. Like all of Science and as discussed in Chapter 2 they involve uncertainty. It is this uncertainty which leads to them being controversial particularly when used to drive Government policy. They involve assumptions and commonly are used to guide how a particular outcome might be achieved. The cancelling of School Examinations in 2020 as a result of Covid19 resulted in students'

203   Rowntree PR (1993) 'Climatic models: Changes in Physical Environmental conditions', pp. 13-32 in *Global Climate Change.*

results being estimated using algorithms which were part of a model which had been asked to minimise grade inflation. This resulted in the results for individual students from previously lower performing schools being reduced, and an adverse societal reaction to the use of mathematical models. Again this tended to emphasis the absence of understanding within society of the uncertainty associated with science.

Essentially, we have not understood the relationship between how we live our lives and our use of natural resources. Governments have been asked to modify how business is done. We have been asked to consider how we heat our homes and better insulate our houses. A fundamental issue is the extent to which we have become disconnected from nature. We have forgotten that we are a part of biology and of nature and God's creation. We seem to have been insufficiently aware of the promptings of Wisdom. It's clear that management of the Earth[204] comes with responsibilities for care.[205] The message from Wisdom Literature, exemplified by the account of Creation in Job, remains apposite, and we affirm this responsibility whenever we pray, "Your will be done on earth, as in heaven." If God as Creator sustains and cares for the world all the time, as the scriptures teach,[206] then we must also, in order to love our neighbour as well as for the sake of Creation itself.

In reflecting on this, two recent activities come to mind:

'Faith Action for Nature' is a joint venture between representatives of Churches in Scotland and the Royal Society for the Protection of Birds (RSPB). It is predicated on the notion that Christians needed to be involved with nature to develop approaches to Climate Change. RSPB saw churches as logical partners in promoting awareness of nature and especially of birds. Material centred around the seasons and the principal events of the church year – Christmas, Easter, Pentecost, Creationtide, Harvest – was produced. Church members were caused to reflect on the world outwith the walls of the church and its relationship to seasonal worship within. Church-RSPB Reserve links promoted the use of the Reserves as a place of reflection. (It is of course understood that not all RSPB members are also Christians.)

---

204 Genesis 1: 28.
205 Genesis 2: 15.
206 E.g. Job 38: 1-18 and Luke 12: 24, 27.

Pilgrimage is an ancient activity.[207] It has long been significant within the church, as Chaucer's Canterbury Tales reminds us. Traditionally Pilgrimage encouraged those of faith to follow a route from the past or journey to a site associated with a major figure of faith. Chaucer's pilgrims were travelling from London to Canterbury to visit the site of the martyrdom of Thomas Becket. What makes the story is the variety of reasons the pilgrims had for making the journey and what they learned about themselves and others during the journey. These remain important. Pilgrimage can have other purposes. If the journey is important then what happens during the journey in what is seen and done with others, what is said, are all critical elements.

The Templeton Foundation's 'Scientists in Congregations Programme' which ran from 2014-16 aimed to get members of congregations relating Science issues to faith. As part of this, two Deeside Churches used Pilgrimage to facilitate conversations about the environment. A series of walks were undertaken which were repeated in Spring and Autumn. The routes suggested issues related to agriculture, including the use of traditional and molecular biology-based approaches to crop improvement and the effect of topography on land use. While the routes were not associated with major saints, they were within an area associated with significant Celtic figures and followed long established routes. Much encountered was of recent lineage but many trees were ancient, a reminder that man's time within creation had been short compared to much seen on the walks.

Challenges to being human. Climate Change has challenged our confidence. It has made us reflect on just to what extent are we in control of what is most important to us. We have become more aware of our impact on other species. The Blue Planet TV Programmes emphasised the impact our wide-spread use of plastics, ubiquitous materials made from oil, have on other species both on land and in the sea, including those living thousands of miles from us.

What can we do about it? We are not helpless. We can act and even without returning to a pre-industrialisation climate we can use our accumulated knowledge, our human capital to increase the natural

207 Matthew 2: 1-2.

capital we have depleted.[208] It is beyond the remit of this book to outline a detailed Climate Change recovery plan, but as part of humanity, we can ask: What we might learn from nature?

First, *Sustainability.* In commenting on Deeside Pilgrimages, reference was made to the antiquity of land plants like the mosses. In the past I have studied arbuscular mycorrhizal fungi (AMF). AMF a symbiotic relationship between fungi and most plants have been traced back around 500 Million years. They are sustainable. It can be argued that without this association life on land would not have come about. This speaks to our place in history. We have been around for thousands of years, other organisms for millions. We should also be aware of the role of co-operation, symbiosis, in sustainability. Plants can survive without AMF but are less well-tuned to the environment. AMF need plants for survival. AMF may not speak but 'molecular conversations', particularly about 'who' will do what and 'who' will manage the energy bank account, happen constantly

Second, *Change.* Evolution is a major change. It is driven by selection of the mutations which change our genetic code and by epigenetics. Should we do this for our own species? Should we do this for other species? To what extent are such changes able to be geared to Climate Change.

Third, *Recovery.* Nature can reclaim areas previously colonised by man. e.g. in NW Scotland where a railway which was closed in the 1930's the route of the line remains. The track was removed many years ago but the infrastructure of station platforms, walls etc remain. Vegetation has returned. There are large coniferous trees growing in the centre of what used to be a platform. An area which used to fix and store Carbon but which ceased with the building of the railway infrastructure, once again is fixing and storing carbon.

Fixation of Carbon by plants has a major role in reducing what would otherwise be released into the atmosphere. Preventing the return of this captured carbon to the atmosphere matters. Trees store carbon in their woody infrastructure possibly for centuries. Grassland stores carbon in the soil. Gardeners will be aware of the increase in the height of a lawn over the

208 Atkinson D *et al* (1994) 'The Sustainability of Lowland Management Systems', pp. 9-18 in *Scottish Sustainable Systems Project, Four Case Studies*, Scottish Office Agriculture and Fisheries Department, Edinburgh.

years. This increase is mainly due to an increase in soil organic matter. It's worth noting in passing that churches own large areas of land which could/ can accentuate these processes. The solution to global Climate Change will be the result of many actions.

Conclusions

Climate Change raises inherent and consequential ethical issues. The inherent issues centre around those most severely impacted by the consequences of the changes. The actions in the developed world such as industrialisation have led to increased summer temperatures and damaging rainfall for many in the developing world. Even within developed countries adverse effects have fallen most on the less well off. As in many matters of ethics the balance between the individual and the population at large is key. In the UK the impact of heavy rain in winter 2019/ 2020 fell on individuals in Yorkshire, Derbyshire and Nottinghamshire. Intense rainfall, sheet lightning and thunder, similar to a tropical storm (but happening in Aberdeenshire!) were associated with a fatal train derailment near Stonehaven in August 2020. This, if anything was needed, just re-emphasises that Climate Change continues to be a real threat - and a threat Now! Questions were raised for all of these events as to where responsibility for damage caused by intense rainfall as part of the Climate Change should lie. Should the responsibility for recompense lie with the government or the individual or even in some cases the planners for building on flood plains or unstable terrain?

The story of Noah instanced a situation where human misdeeds resulted in the deaths of humans and other species. What man did wrong impacted on others who had no role in the misdeed. The instructions as to who was to enter the ark made it clear that birds, beasts and crawling things were being valued as much as were Noah and his family. Alongside the current background focus in 2020 of Extinction Rebellion and Greta Thunberg,[209] equal priority being given to 'species other than us' is critical. Climate Change will have many effects on food production and so famine in some areas of the world is likely. In such situations people will need

---

209 A Swedish teenager who rose to global prominence as a result of her campaigns to demand urgent effective action from world leaders to address Climate Change before it was too late.

to be fed and so a food policy which plans for this is important. Joseph emphasises that such policies can have economic consequences and can result in major shifts in the ownership of assets and in power relationships between individuals and nations. Fairness is a key issue.

Where do we go from here? Climate Change is changing the world as we have known it. We can mitigate its effects and hopefully reduce its impact. The extent to which we do this will influence how much change is needed. In a very real sense what will happen is not within our control. We can anticipate and we can reflect on why this is happening. In all of this there is a warning about our use of new knowledge and the importance of questioning. The Climate Change issue will be with us for decades to come. There will be technical solutions. Carbon capture and storage is back on the agenda. Our key decision will be the dilemma of setting a balance between changing our lifestyles and thus emitting less CO_2 and finding technical fixes to allow business as usual. Agriculture and food will be a special case. It is a world-wide activity. It generates greenhouse gases but also fixes CO_2. Would all of us going vegetarian help? But not all land is suitable for crop production and it could reduce long term soil carbon storage. The issues are complex. There are few off-the-shelf solutions. There are no easy answers.

Chapter 11
A Miscellany of Thoughts

In this book, developments in the biological Sciences with implications for human society, and for how we journey with Scripture, have been reviewed. The very real possibility of being able to re-imagine our genetics and so our identity as a species results in challenges which to date have largely been the territory of Science Fiction. This raises questions which have floated around in discussions over the years, but not as questions urgently needing hard answers. We have viewed these developments in this book through the lens of the question *'What does it Mean to be Human?'* We have reached a decision time. We need to consider. Do we really have the wisdom to make lasting changes to the genetic makeup of our species? We may well, especially in a post Covid19 era, want to answer, *No*. Do we understand its implications both socially and biologically? All developments happen in a context and will be developed, or not, within a context. Context is vital.

Currently the major drivers across the world seem to be Climate Change and Covid19. Both have challenged people's sense of being in control of the things most important to our survival. We seem to have lost the ability to predict in a timely manner but most of all we have lost the confidence that we thought that we had, to act with 'certainty'. However, in parallel with this, there is a growing awareness of the importance of equality and that global forces impact unevenly between different parts of the world, and within a country on different individuals and groups. This has long been acknowledged in relation to Climate Change but is now becoming apparent in relation to the impact of Covid19. Covid19 has hit disproportionately those from BAME communities and those in fragile employments which meant that they needed to work, ill or not. It has also disproportionately impacted on older people. It has asked hard questions about the allocation of resources in health care such as the distribution of DNR forms to patients with health care issues so as to allow the focus to be on younger patients with a better chance of survival. It has asked who might benefit from future genetic changes?

Will any benefits which result from all that might be done with Genome Editing be unevenly distributed? Will this become another area of inequality? Would we want to use such methods to aid the BAME community or has the disproportionate impact of Covid19 been all about social structures and living conditions, not genetics? Will benefits really be available to all? All lead us to reflect on matters of life and death and the relation between them and how we function as both individuals and 'Society'.

Scotland. The genetic Journey of the people of Scotland reminds us of interactions between climate, health and the development of society.[210] The mini Ice Ages which occurred between 1300 and 1850 raised similar issues to some of the concerns around Climate Change. Robert the Bruce's failure to take Carlisle in 1315 was largely a consequence of a climate change and the resulting mud around the city walls of Carlisle. The absence of adequate sunshine in that year and the next caused famine and resulted in the death of the old and unwell and then of children. The impact of the mini Ice Age was made worse by the arrival of the Black Death in 1349. An attempt to invade England from Galashiels had to be abandoned as a result of the start of the plague brought to Scotland by imported mercenaries. Over the years up to 1455, more than a third of the population of Scotland was lost. Agriculture declined and with it, trade required a new 'normal'. This historic journey has a clear resemblance to the Covid19 pandemic in which we currently find ourselves. Discussion of a Science linked approach reminds us of past limitations resulting from an over-emphasis on this as primary driver and its continuing consequences. It focuses our attention on Wisdom.

Coping with Uncertainty

Wisdom leads us back to how we reconcile the unexpected and the ways in which the unexpected may impact differentially on different groups within any society. Any new technology if widely adopted has the potential to create winners and losers. This has ever been the case. A new

---

210 Moffat A and Wilson JF (2011) *The Scots: A genetic journey*, Birlinn, Edinburgh.

approach or skill requirement can result in some being advantaged at the expense of others. Variations among people may give societies as a whole resilience and the ability to adapt. This would not necessarily be true of all individuals. This returns us to the thought which has previously been expressed in this book that what may be good for society as a whole is rarely good for all individuals. Earlier in the book the question is asked as to whether Genome Editing might be used to move humanity as a whole towards a new 'normal' by eliminating what might be viewed as disabilities. This again asks what positive value we as a society place on 'difference'? It asks how committed we are to equality. The evidence from how we cope with illnesses such as the Black death, AIDS and Covid19 suggests that it's not always something we find easy. The same would be true of how society has reacted to LGBT and BAME people in the recent past.

This book has been written during the Covid19 Lockdown and what I have written has been hugely affected by a continuing discussion with my partner Margaret who has identified many of the issues I have discussed here with issues linked to equality and to how we treat each other. This being the case it seemed right to complete the book with a reflection, in prose and verse which she produced on life as it has been, as it is currently and which could be different in the future but only if we have the confidence to want something different.

From the Side-lines . . .[211]

Margaret comments, *"My agreement re involvement with this book written by David was purely to proof-read it – strangely a task I find enjoyable!*

As he says, we had many interesting and challenging discussions along the way because David and I, as individuals, definitely approach the religious correlations from totally different standpoints. However, reading about the new bioscience developments has for me been enlightening and thought provoking. Alongside all that, as is my way, I have made many comments on the social injustices and consequences exposed by the Covid19 virus and how it has impacted all our lives during this strange period of enforced Lockdown, and, for whatever reason best known to himself, David has chosen to include

---

211 Reflections and poem here by Margaret Hadley.

here some of my thoughts – although they are far outwith my initial job description!

Was Second Hand, Now First Hand. *All of us have a passing awareness of floods, famines, tsunamis, the senseless wars rooted in religious differences or power grabs, but on the whole that awareness has been of a kind that makes us feel these things happen to other peoples, in other places. Also, even with the wonder of awareness-raising aspects like TV and 24/7 rolling News, unless you are actually 'in the eye of the storm', the horrors were second hand with the result a de-sensitization to their effects becomes quite normal. Not so today, now it's first hand as we live and die as Covid19 sweeps across the whole world. Disaster movies have conditioned us to it 'all coming right in the end' – but this is different. At the time of writing, there is no Knight in shining armour riding to our rescue, no magic bullet to wipe out this invisible enemy – each one of us is at risk, vulnerable. The world has become a village where individual life and death is totally bound up with each and every one of our individual 'village' neighbours. As the death toll rises daily our only weapons – testing, lockdowns, social isolation and theoretical vaccines – give little protection or certainty against the indiscriminate progress of this virus as it rampages with no respect for borders, ethnicity or age.*

The vulnerability of 'being human' has seldom been so stark, as physical, mental and social health are ripped apart – we wait and watch in fear. The glib phrase 'life will never be the same again' will be true, not a mere fridge magnet trite phrase the likes of which we have lived by for so long. But will humankind change? Can humankind change? Will all our scientific knowhow help us to aim for a better world where the haves / have-nots societies are replaced by a fairer distribution of, and access to the world's wealth and resources? Or, will what it means to be human just revert to /derive from the circumstances of our birth as before, i.e. the lottery of genetics, geography and parental chance?

The WHO definition of HEALTH is represented as an equilateral triangle – i.e. one in which all the sides are equal and interdependent and these sides are labelled Physical/ Social/ Mental and Emotional respectively, and this symbolises the need for these 'sides' in an individual to remain equal and stable to maintain health and well-being.

With this definition in mind it is obvious there will be long term effects on individuals and societies as a result of the myriad of unusual and sometimes traumatic life experiences associated with the Covid19 pandemic. Moreover, for every one of us in the world today, it is like living in a Venn diagram where the overlapping circles of Climate Change, the Pandemic, Economic disruption, Inequalities, Refugees, Wars, Racial Discrimination all rage around us and we, sitting centre circle , can only look on and hope."

BEING HUMAN

Without breath we have no life

Without respect we have no self esteem

Without the basics we have no hope

Without hope we have nothing in the lottery of life

#WIMTBH 2020

Essentially life is a lottery – a roulette wheel of chances

Chance happenings/ chance opportunities / chance genetic packages

Do we have choices or is life one long or short pre-destined plan?

Why do inequalities and discrimination blight so many lives?

Why do privilege and expectations favour the few in a world of 7.6bn?

Can overstretched Health Services cope with new extra demands?

As I reflect on the question of what it means to be human, two statements I heard on the Today programme (27/6/20) stuck in my mind:

'We are at the tipping point of our values system'

'At this moment Britain is a tinderbox of inequalities'

*"Surely the world and all its competing faiths cannot blindly go on as before. Were the new **3 Rs** referred to in Chapter 9 to be adhered to we would all show more **Respect** for our fellow humans, we should see the need for more equality in terms of **Rights** , and we would be taking **Responsibility** more seriously in relation to Climate Change/ our behaviour/ our consumerism – all of which would certainly benefit human life around us."*

Last Word Goes to David!

I am an ardent listener to the BBC Radio 4 Today Programme. On the morning of 27th August 2020 three items, coming almost back to back, captured my attention.

First, the England cricketer James Anderson, who had recently become the first Fast Bowler to take 600 Test wickets, commented on the strides being made to improve fitness in sport. He explained the ways in which different sports were now co-operating to better understand how increased fitness and performance could be achieved. This prompted a reflection about sport. Could Genome Editing of cells, removed, edited and replaced in athletes, increase performance? Might the explicit use of agents to trigger epigenetic responses which affect muscles, then impact fitness or stamina?

The second item was from the mother of a young boy who suffers from a muscle wasting disease and, prior to Covid19, he had been undergoing tests in his local hospital so as to identify whether he would benefit from an experimental drug. All of this came to an end with Covid19 when the NHS decided to focus on people with the virus. The mother hoped that it would not now be too late for him, for the treatment to be given.

In the third item Sir Paul Nurse, the director of the Crick Institute, lamented the fall-off in the finance available for medical research as a result of a very significant decline in the income from people's donations to medical Charities resulting from the cancelation of charity events and the closing of charity shops following Lockdown brought about by Covid19. He stressed the hitherto strength of the UK in medical research, something which was now under threat as a result of the drying up of this funding stream, and which could subsequently restrict research.

I am conscious that much of the material presented here has come from secular sources. Most of the issues, although raising profound ethical challenges, represent challenges for the whole of society. So, do people of Faith have a distinct contribution to make? If they do what is it? Part of this must relate to the common response to a problem which says, 'If only I had known then what I know now I wouldn't have done that'. This has ever been the case. The Wisdom Books are a theological version of the practical advice 'measure twice cut once'. Bringing to bear the Wisdom from Scripture is a very real contribution to be made by people of faith. The Bible is not a medical text book but the 'Healing Miracles' performed by Jesus tell us much about the human condition in sickness and in health. They emphasise that health is just so much more than not being ill. This has ever been an issue for the NHS. People who cannot be cured of an illness seem to fall outwith their model. Wisdom helps us to reflect on its complexity and on the extent to which health goes beyond mere matters of surgery or pharmaceuticals.

More important than this is the opportunity for Christians to link discussion of these new technologies to the long journey of humanity's learning more and growing closer to God. Scripture has constantly been reinterpreted as the world around us has changed. Deeper understanding was engendered by more and more instances of the out-working of God's purposes. These important developments need to be seen as a way of continuing such a process and further enhancing our traditions. The closing words of Matthew's Gospel[212] provide a practical course of action related to such problems. For those who suggest that Jesus did not in his teaching ministry refer to issues of this type there is help from the closing words of John's Gospel.

> *There is much else that Jesus did. If it were to be recorded in detail, I suppose the world could not hold the books that would be written.* (John 21: 25)

'What does it mean to be Human' is at the heart of Scripture and tradition. For Christians this has to involve knowledge and love of God. Answering the question will always be important and perhaps particularly now when both making major changes to humanity becomes a real practical option and coping with the threat of a pandemic is reshaping the world.

Covid19 and its wider impact has become so dominant to national thinking during 2020 that it almost asks the question as to whether there is any point in discussing other biology-based issues such as the ones covered here. Are they not just too trivial at this time? Covid19 has shown up our inability to deal with issues which have at their heart genetics. This is linked to who has suffered most? It has also asked whether we

---

212 Matthew 28: 18-20.

really are capable of learning from the past? It has asked about our ability to exercise Wisdom. How good are we at deciding things which will impact for generations? With this as background do we really have the wisdom to begin making fundamental long-term changes to our own genetic make-up. Do we really know how we would want to evolve? We could, but would this be wise?

Chapter 12

Finally: The Science That Went Before

The principal subjects which are discussed in this Book relate to our ability to manipulate the human and other genomes and some of the consequences for our society of being able to do that. We have discussed the development of the recently discovered method used to modify genomes and issues around CRISPR/Cas9. Science is both recursive and an evolving process. All current developments and discoveries have their roots in past developments. The aim here was to discuss some of the biological issues of today, to look at them through the eyes of people asking basic philosophical and faith-related questions. This final chapter is an optional read for those who would like to have more detail of the Science. In Chapter 2 the question of what is Science was addressed. It seems important to re-emphasise some key issues. Fundamentally all scientific conclusions and understandings are provisional. Science is not monolithic – scientists disagree and argue. Some advances are important not for their novelty as Science but because they alter public perception and thus widen related aspects of being human. Topics are organised here on the basis of when the discovery was made or when it became an issue.

Evolution 1859. Evolution and Creation have long been controversial for some members of the church and so, as Adam is mentioned in Chapter 2, it seemed important to comment here about the relationship between the metaphorical exploration of history presented in the Bible's Book entitled Genesis and the scientific explanation. The basics of the Concept of Evolution were spelt out by Charles Darwin in his book ' The Origin of Species' which was first published in 1859.[213] The revolutionary theory[214]

---

213 Darwin CR (1859) *The Origin of Species*, Wordsworth Classics of World Literature, 1998.

214 Ellis J (2010) 'Two ways of explaining the world', pp. 1-5 in *How Science Works: Evolution*, Springer, Dordrecht.

advanced in that book resulted in part from Darwin's observations during his voyage on HMS Beagle between 1831 and 1836.[215] A number of chapters in that book contain reference to material from the first book of the Bible, Genesis. The descriptions given in Genesis are essentially of the relationship between the world and all its life and God. Nothing there automatically leads to the conclusion that the world, as it was at the time of writing Genesis, had all been created at one time, an idea that would make the Book of Genesis incompatible with the evolutionary theory developed by Darwin. The fossil record which became clearer over the latter years of the second Christian millennium, indicated that in the past there had been living organisms which were no longer extant. Darwin provided an explanation for the way in which change could have occurred slowly and the forces which were driving it. He postulated how forces that govern survival could affect life and lead to the survival of the fittest and through such a mechanism cause developmental change, i.e. evolution. The discovery of the structure of DNA in 1953 provided a molecular mechanism by which the theory of Darwinian Evolution could have come about. The history of the debate over evolution shows that people take time to reconcile tradition with emerging scientific concepts.[216] Where this book refers to Creation it is taken to be consistent with a darwinian version of evolution.

Viruses 1922. Viruses were discovered earlier than 1922 but their structure was not seen until the electron microscope became available to biologists in the 1940's. Viruses were first identified in 1898 in plants. The name was derived from the Latin for *poison* and was at that time used to describe a filterable agent smaller than a bacterium that was capable of causing diseases in plants and animals. 1922 represents the date of the first successful attempts to purify the poxvirus.[217] Viruses are the smallest organised infective structures capable of replicating in living cells. The Nobel Laurate Peter Medawar described a virus as being a piece of bad news wrapped in a protein. A typical virus consists of coiled genetic material, usually RNA, in a protective protein coat and commonly a lipid envelope. They survive by invading cells and replicating themselves. Their

215 Darwin CR (1839) *The Voyage of the Beagle*, Vintage, London 2009.

216 Spanner DC (1965) *Creation and Evolution,* Falcon Books, London.

217 Horne R (1978) *The structure and function of viruses*, Studies in Biology no 95, Edward Arnold, London.

inability to replicate or produce their own energy puts them somewhere between life and the molecular world. Coronaviruses have spiked proteins on their surface which fit into receptors already present on the surface of a human cell which then allows them to enter the cell.

They therefore contain the genetic material necessary for replicating identical progeny within a host cell. That material can be either DNA or RNA which is protected by a protein or lipoprotein coat. These materials are important for the infection process. When assembly of virus progeny within a cell is complete the cell dies and releases a packaged structure which may then contact a new host. By the 1920s we were clear that a range of viruses existed and were the cause of the Spanish Flu. Currently there are over 2,000 recognised viruses which include Hepatitis B, the Rhinoviruses responsible for the common cold and HIV. Coronaviruses are a family that infect many species, including humans.

Cohort Studies 1946. In 1946 a study began in the UK of a cohort of 13,687 children all born in the week 3-9 March, which continues to this day.[218] The initial size of the group was reduced to the more manageable size of 5,362. The cohort has facilitated studies of the impact of post Second World War societal changes, such as the NHS and improved education, on health and survival. It has been invaluable to human epidemiology. The cohort has been used to find out where adverse conditions in life have affected health or susceptibility to infection by a disease. This approach followed one begun in the 1830's by William Farr. In 1841 he showed that 27% of 'paupers' died in asylums.[219] This has similarities with the deaths caused recently by Covid19 in care homes.

HeLa Cells 1951. HeLa is a reference to cells that were grown from a tumour in the cervix of Henrietta Lacks who died in 1951.[220] The history of these cells is important to the development of cell-culture techniques, and the related molecular biology, and to our understanding of how cells differentiate. In 1951 the culture of human cells was in its infancy. During an operation to remove a tumour from Henrietta, a slice of the tumour was removed for subsequent culture. At that time the ability to culture cells

---

218 Helen Pearson (2016) *The life Project*, Allen Lane, London.

219 Farr W (1841) *Report on the Mortality of Lunatics*, Proceedings of the Statistical Society of London.

220 Rebecca Skloot (2010) *The Immortal Life of Henrietta Lacks*, Macmillan, London.

and to maintain a cell culture was rare. Unusually Henrietta's cells were successfully cultured and multiplied at great speed so that the number of them doubled on a daily basis. They became the first immortal human cells. Cell cultures were sent around the world principally for use in Cancer research programmes. They were used in drug testing and were important for research on Polio. This work resulted in the development of a factory for producing cells needed as part of a test for Polio. The factory was built within months of Henrietta's death and produced around 6 trillion cells per week. They have had a key role in research on human viruses and in our understanding of genetics. The fact that we have 46 chromosomes in our genome was first discovered using HeLa cells.

The use of HeLa cells raised key questions about Science, ethics, race and about where faith is involved. The attitudes towards people of colour in 1950's US society determined how Henrietta was treated, the limited care she received and the continued lack of attempts to seek consent for what was to happen to her cells. Doctors believed it was best not to upset patients with information. HeLa cells are therefore a good example to start our discussion on scientific results from a faith perspective. Rebecca Skloot[221] who wrote about the history of HeLa cells commented that Henrietta's daughter Deborah and she had grown up in very different cultures. Rebecca was white and agnostic, while Deborah was a very religious black Christian who believed that her mother's spirit continued to live on in her cells and that they had the power to influence the life of anyone who had contact with them.

Deborah recalled her mother in the following ways:

Henrietta died in 1951. She is remembered because doctors at John Hopkin's Hospital in Baltimore took cells from her before she died. When not in a frozen state, Henrietta's cells are still livin, continue multiplyin, growin and spreadin.

She reflects that whenever she sees a physician they have a habit of reminding her of the role that her mother's cells have had in the development of her blood pressure medicine and her anti-depressant pills, and of the amount of critical science which would never have happened without the role played by her mother Henrietta's cells.

---

221 Rebecca Skloot (2010) *ibid.*

Also, the family were not consulted about the use of her mother's cells which, over the years, have made many people significant riches. As a result, Deborah also thinks how ironical it is that since her mother has done so much to benefit medical science, why is it that today she and her family cannot afford to see a doctor?

Rebecca quotes Deborah in the following terms: 'The story of Henrietta Lacks warns us that individuals and wider society may benefit differently from developments in Science.'

Polio Vaccination 1952. The first vaccine was developed by Jenner in 1796 against the Smallpox disease. Material from someone infected with the related Cowpox was inoculated into the skin. The basic theory was then, and remains, that if a patient at risk is exposed to key features of a virus or bacterium, usually elements of its protein coat that are called antigens, the body will learn to recognise them as hostile and will, in response, produce antibodies which will then provide protection against the disease-causing virus or bacteria for an extended period. Vaccines were developed at a time of little awareness of the immunological mechanism. The vaccine works with the body's natural defence mechanisms. It makes use of the white cells in our blood that are the primary means by which we respond to infection. There are three major types of white blood cells:

1 Macrophages that digest pathogens and dying host cells. They expose the pathogen's signature antigens which the body recognises and then stimulates the production of antibodies.

2 B-lymphocytes that produce the antibodies that attack the antigen.

3 T-lymphocytes (T Cells) that attack the cells in the body which have been infected. T Cells act as memory cells. T Cells had a key role in the story of Layla Richards which we discuss in Chapter 5. They are involved in the overreaction of our defence mechanism, something which has been linked to some deaths from Covid19.

By the late 1940's large scale facilities existed for the production of vaccines for Smallpox, Diphtheria, Tetanus, and Whooping cough. The most pressing need in the 1950s was for a vaccine to protect against Polio, Infantile Paralysis. A vaccine for Polio was developed in 1952 by Jonas Salk and was in commercial production by the mid 1950's. Since then vaccination has been the health measure of choice for protecting against viral diseases. Successful development of the Polio vaccine was critically dependant on the use of HeLa cells. Where a high proportion of the population has been vaccinated then 'Herd Immunity' has a protective role for the population as a whole, including those not vaccinated: the number of infectable hosts falls to a low number and the easy spread of the pathogen is prevented.

With the advent of Covid19 the role and availability of vaccination has become of significant public interest. The ability to develop a vaccine is uncertain. HIV/AIDS spread as a significant illness in the 1970s but as yet an effective vaccine against it has not been developed. The priority, or perhaps absence of priority, for developing a vaccine against it may be linked to AIDs being associated originally with homosexuality, and its prevalence in the developing world.[222]

DNA 1953. 'DNA' is an abbreviation which has passed into common usage. It carries the essence of who we are and what characteristics we pass on to our children. It has become a metaphor for fundamental qualities that determine almost everything. In 1953 the structure of the means of genetic transfer, the DNA molecule, was published having been discovered by Francis Crick, James Watson, Maurice Wilkins and Rosalind Franklin. Its double helix, with two strands which run in opposite directions, which code for genetic information (genes) was discovered to have a sequence of chemical letters which replicate and pass on information from cell to cell. Each strand has a backbone of alternating sugar and phosphate groups that support sequences of four possible base pairs usually abbreviated as A, T, C, or G. Chemically A on one strand is able to pair with T on the other strand. Similarly, C on one strand can pair with G on the other. This means that the base on one strand, at the time of replication, would specify the base opposite on the other strand. This suggested exactly how strands could be precisely replicated. The DNA molecule is able to split into 2 strands by choosing opposite bases to build them and then reconstruct the missing opposite strand, copies which are passed on to daughter cells. Cells read the sequence within a gene and this information allows cells to specify and build proteins. The discovery of this mechanism was the start of attempts to understand how the DNA we inherit from our parents influences our

---

222 Shilts R (2011) *And the Band Played On: Politics, People and the AIDS Epidemic,* Souvenir Press, London.

susceptibility to disease. It allowed the identification of instances where the mutation of just a single gene could be responsible for a disease.

Organ transplantation 1954. The first successful kidney transplantation took place in Boston USA in 1954. Liver, heart and pancreas transplants followed in the 1960's and transplantation of lungs in the 1980's. Continuing to develop this as an approach could be considered to be an alternative to the approach of genome therapy. The shortage of organs available for transplant led to the suggestion of using transgenic pigs as a source of human transplants. The shortage of organs has also led to an assumption of *presumed consent* in some countries (including, to date, parts of the UK), i.e. organs can be taken unless the person who has died has previously put their name on a Register to state that they do not wish this transplant to happen – a Regulation which seems to contradict the terms of what was originally called *Organ Donation*, a term derived from the Latin word for 'gift'!

Epigenetics 1957. Embryonic cells begin with unlimited potential: They can turn into any type of cell. The cells of an embryo differentiate as they age and with time it becomes progressively harder to induce them to become a different type of cell. Interestingly differentiated cells can be de-programmed and then re-programmed. Genes that have ceased to work can be re-activated. Genes which are part of the genome can be switched off either permanently or for a long period. Epigenetics is the study of just how gene-regulating attachments, the epigenetic signature, are emplaced and removed. Differentiated cells are normally epigenetically modified at a molecular level; this is why skin cells remain skin cells, and it is important that they do. For cells to be deprogrammed the epigenetic signature needs to be removed so that the cell once again becomes pluripotent. How we function is thus not merely a matter of the genome we are born with but is also a product of this switching process. Some kinds of switching happen on a permanent basis while other elements are impacted by the environment.

So how does this switch work? What is the mechanism? The 'naked gene' consists of a short length of DNA as a double helix. Our genes' DNA is however usually covered by a variety of other organic molecules, which are chemically attached. These include histones and other specialised proteins such as the polycombe protein complex. Whether the bases have or have not an attached Methyl (CH4) group is also important. These chemical attachments make genes more or less active, polycombes can remodel chromatin and silence genes. These chemical processes, which affect gene functioning, can be changed by hormones such as oestrogen. Such changes are the basis of the interaction of the genetic code with our environment and thus augments the nurture factor.

RNA 1961. RNA was identified in the 19th century but its structure was unclear until 1961 when Messenger RNA (mRNA), with its role in gene regulation was discovered. Transfer RNA (tRNA), reads the code on the mRNA to specify which amino acids are joined in sequence to build the required protein molecule. Ribosomal RNA (rRNA) had been known since the mid 1950's. RNA carries the message from DNA to make proteins. After the discovery that the sequence of bases on DNA coded its genetic information, the key question became how is that information turned into biological functioning? m-RNA is like a tape-recording which copies information from DNA and carries that information to the ribosome which reads the information and follows its instruction to assemble the protein. RNA is able to function both as a repository of genetic instruction and as a chemically reactive molecule able. It is able to change its shape and fold into three dimensional structures more complex than the DNA double helix.

In Vitro Fertilisation 1978. The development of In Vitro Fertilisation (IVF) followed the introduction of artificial insemination by husband (AIH) and artificial insemination by donor (AID) as treatments for infertility. It was found to be possible to fertilise a human egg outwith the body and in 1978 Louise Brown was born England. By 2006 over 3 million babies worldwide had been born using this technology. In Denmark it has been estimated that as many as 4-5% of the population have involved the use of IVF. However even today the success rate remains 15-30%. The costs of producing children in this way remain substantial.[223] The technique has given laboratory access to a supply of human embryos for research purposes

IVF has increased the complexity of thinking about the process of producing a child. This method can now be seen to have four components:

---

223   Wyatt J (2009) 'Reproductive technology and the start of life', pp. 83-106, in *Matters of Life and Death*, Intervarsity Press, London.

1) An egg
2) A sperm
3) a womb and
4) one or more care-givers post birth.

All possible combinations and permutations of these elements are possible, e.g. a child may have, separately, a genetic mother, a carrying mother and a caring mother. Technically the process is simple: A hormonal treatment induces the female partner to super-ovulate to produce 5-20 eggs rather than 1. The eggs are harvested, incubated and mixed with sperm from a donor. If all has gone well then over the next 3-5 days the size of each embryo increases from one cell to around 50, a blastocyst. At this point one or more embryos are selected for implantation. Increasing the number of embryos implanted increases the chance of a successful pregnancy, but also of multiple pregnancies. Embryos can be stored frozen for a number of years.

The success of the IVF process has raised the question of what is to be done with the 'spare' frozen embryos. The options would seem to be:

1) freeze them for later use

2) donate them to another woman

3) donate them for use in research which ultimately will result in embryo destruction

4) discard them immediately.

The third and fourth options raise questions around when does life begin and question whether embryos are a person in their own right. These complexities led to the formation of the Human Fertilisation and Embryology Authority (HFEA) and the 1990 Human Fertilisation and Embryology Act. Dilemmas at the beginning of life are commonly a matter of significant personal pain. This is true of infertility: the lack of a baby who is desperately wanted. Modern society and churches are family oriented so experiencing infertility can lead to feelings of isolation. This was ever so.[224]

The structure of Ribosomes 1980. RNA had been known before this date but around this time it was crystallised, a key step to understanding its structure and function and how ribosomes worked.[225] Ribosomes are where

224 1 Samuel 1: 11-17.
225 Ramakrishnan V (2018) *Gene Machine: The race to decipher the secrets of the Ribosome*, One World, London.

mRNA is read and proteins made. Every cell has thousands of ribosomes. They are large in molecular terms, containing around 50 proteins and 3 distinct pieces of RNA (rRNA). The ribosome can bind mRNA and stitch together the amino acids brought by tRNA into a protein.

GM Crops 1995. The ability to cut, copy and paste genes was critical to both the production of GM crops in the 1990's and to the techniques linked to Genome Editing with systems such as CRISPR/Cas9.[226] DNA molecules are isolated from an originating organism (Cut) copied to produce a useable quantity commonly in a bacterial system (Copying) It is then introduced into the DNA of a recipient organism (Paste).[227] Doing this needs the use of an enzyme which is part of the natural defence mechanism of bacteria i.e. Restriction Endonucleases, which cut DNA at specified places. Each of these recognises a short stretch of DNA and makes a cut on either side of it. They can be used to cut and join DNA from different sources; this process is the basis of recombinant genetic sequence technology. Sequences are multiplied many times before being introduced into the intended host (cloning). The new gene is attached to a vector which multiplies and distributes the new gene sequence. The Polymerase Chain Reaction (PCR) can also be used to make copies of gene sequences.

Glyphosate resistant Soya was introduced in early 1995 and GM tomato paste later that same year. The initial introduction of GM crops as a Tomato Paste went well – tins were labelled as GM. When Monsanto announced that its GM modified Soya Bean and Oil Seed Rape products would not be labelled thus, there was a major public revolt in Europe.

Gene transfer in animals involves the direct injection of copies of a recombinant gene into the cell nucleus of an early embryo (similar to IVF). Typically, the success rate results in 10-20% of eggs leading to viable young, but with only around 1% carrying the new gene. As the new gene will have integrated into only one of the chromosomes in a pair, only half of later offspring will carry the transformation.

---

226 Doudna J and Sternberg S (2017) *A Crack in Creation: The new power to control evolution*, Bodley Head , London. Carey N (2019) *Hacking the Code of Life. How gene editing will rewrite our futures*, Icon Books, London.

227 Bruce D and Bruce A (1998) 'Explaining Genetic Engineering and its Uses', pp. 1-29 in *Engineering Genesis*, Earthscan, London.

Stem Cells 1997. Stem cells are of two types. One type can produce any type of cell - *totipotent* cells such as *Embryonic* stem cells which must be able to produce any type of cell found in the mature human body. There are also stem cells with more limited abilities - *pluripotent* cells, which allow the production of one or a limited range of cell types. The cells in the umbilical cord, skin and bone marrow can produce only cord cells, skin cells or blood cells. It is important that this is the case. If such cells are re-programmed, other than for organ or tissue repair, the results are dangerous; uncontrolled cell re-programming is the basis of cancer. When Henrietta Lacks cervix began to produce not the cells that she needed to line her cervix, but the cancerous cells, which are now known as HeLa cells (see HeLa cells above), they subsequently invaded other organs in her body with fatal results.

Cells in the organs in the human body frequently need to be replaced. When this replacement doesn't occur naturally, injecting stem cells can be an appropriate treatment. Over 70 different therapies based around stem cells are now relatively common, such as bone marrow transplants. All of these therapies use adult pluripotent stem cells.[228] It has been possible to re-programme some pluripotent cells e.g. skin stem cells so that they can produce a wider range of cell types. If the initial cells are derived from the intended host then this ancestry will avoid rejection. In the UK there has been considerable pressure to make it legally easier to use stem cells derived from human embryos.

Cloning 1997. Cloning involves the transfer of nuclei between individuals of the same species.[229] Genetic material is removed from the unfertilised egg and is replaced by the genetic material of the donor cell. This process involves two cells, an unfertilised egg and a donor cell. Dolly, the sheep, was born from cells derived from the mammary gland of an adult sheep. Usually the fertilisation of an egg is followed by cell divisions and differentiation into an early embryo and then into all the cell types needed for the adult animal. The assumption was that once a cell had differentiated, its cell type was set. It was not possible for it to forget what

228 Wyatt J (2009) 'Regenerative Medicine and Embryonic Stem Cells', pp. 125-128, in *Matters of Life and Death.*.

229 Wilmut I and Bruce D (1998) 'Dolly Mixture: Cloning by nuclear transfer to improve genetic engineering in animals', pp. 71-76, in *Engineering Genesis*.

type of cell it had been / was and begin again. The birth of Dolly indicated that this was possible. A nucleus from an older cell could be transferred successfully and that transfer of a nucleus to the cytoplasm of the egg could prompt regeneration so that such a transformed egg could then be brought to term.

The Human Genome 2001. The human genome was sequenced in 2001. It consists of around 3 billion letters. Knowledge of the normal sequences in the human genome has allowed the identification of over 4,000 DNA mutations that can cause genetic diseases. CRISPR/Cas9 provides the ability to make changes in our DNA and with enough sensitivity to be able to change just a single base pair if that is where the problem lies and that change is what is needed for repair.

Genome Editing 2008. This is now most commonly done using CRISPR/ Cas9 but there were earlier approaches which brought about similar end results, albeit less effectively. Zinc finger nucleases (ZFN) can be used to cut DNA and thus enabled homologous re-combinations to be produced. They could be used in some animals and a number of plants such as tobacco and corn, and showed that DNA double-strand breaks promoted efficient homologous recombination. ZFNs were not programmable enough to be a multipurpose tool and so were supplanted by Transcription Activator Like Effectors (TALEs) which were similar in construction to ZFNs and led to a combination of the two TALE Nucleases (TALENs) which were effective at initiating gene editing inside cells. TALENs were however rapidly over taken by CRISPR technology[230] TALEN was, interestingly, the technology which led to the modified T cells which were to save the life of Layla Richards (Chapter 5).

CRISPR 2009. CRISPR has become so important to Genome Editing that we give it a section of its own. Jenifer Doudna began work on CRISPR in 2006 but establishing its full potential took time. CRISPR is the abbreviation used for *Clustered Regularly Interspaced Short Palindromic Repeats*. Short repeats of around 30 base pairs of DNA are interspaced with unique DNA sequences; all clustered in a particular region of a chromosome. The repeats were similar regardless of the direction from which they were read; palindromes (like the name HannaH). DNA sequences from bacterial populations showed that almost every cell had a different CRISPR array as a

230 Doudna J and Sternberg S (2017).

result of the unique sequences between the repeats. This was very unusual as the rest of the DNA in these cells was almost identical. CRISPRs are found in almost all prokaryotes and many of the unique DNA sequences between the spacers were matches for known viral DNA sequences. CRISPR seemed to be part of a system which enabled bacteria to fend off viruses. Viruses which infect bacteria are known as Bacteriophages (abbreviated to phage; i.e. Eater of bacteria). Bacteria have an 'immune' system to guard against phages. They use restriction endonucleases to cut apart viral DNA. Phages are ubiquitous and the most prevalent biological entity on the planet. The best estimate is that there are around 10^{31} (i.e. for non-scientists that is 10 to the power of 31) phages on earth and in the oceans alone. Phages are responsible for the death of 40% of bacteria every day. The CRISPR sequence in bacteria is always associated with a set of genes which are distinct and different. These CRISPR-associated genes (cas genes) code for specialist enzymes whose role seems either to be to unzip DNA or to slice up DNA or RNA. RNA coded for, by DNA, co-ordinates the recognition and destruction phases of antiviral responses. Both CRISPR RNA and an additional type of RNA, tracr RNA are needed for functioning. There are a number of cas genes but Cas9 seems to have special properties and to be particularly effective at cutting DNA.

Covid 19 and other Corona Viruses. Since 2002 two new coronaviruses that can infect humans and result in more severe disease have appeared – Severe Acute Respiratory Syndrome (SARS) and Middle East Respiratory Syndrome (MERS) coronaviruses. Both SARS and MERS coronaviruses are thought to have originated in animals. They are transmitted via droplets in coughs and sneezes. On 31st December 2019, Chinese authorities notified the World Health Organisation of an outbreak of viral pneumonia in Wuhan City. A study published in 'Nature' suggested that the novel coronavirus originated in bats with another species serving as an intermediate host. Wildlife markets put people and live and dead animals in close contact, so facilitating inter-species transfers. On 10th February, the WHO named the disease caused by the novel coronavirus COVID-19. The virus itself has been named SARS-CoV-2. It is the same species as SARS but a different strain.

As with SARS, the spikes of SARS-CoV-2 bind to a receptor on human cells called angiotensin-converting enzyme 2 (ACE2). Once bound, the spike proteins undergo a structural change that enables the viral membrane to fuse with the cell membrane and insert genetic material, its RNA, into the cell. The cell assumes that the viral RNA is a product of its own DNA and begins to produce copies of the viral RNA which ultimately kills the host cell and releases the virus to infect other host cells. In severely impacted hosts the immune system may respond by producing Cytokine proteins which draw in T cells, which kill off infected cells, to the site of the infection. An over-production of Cytokines can result in the T cells killing healthy cells and so sometimes leading to the death of the patient.

Studies of the SARS-CoV-2 spike found it to be particularly aggressive. This may enable it to spread more easily from person to person than SARS, which caused around 8,000 cases of respiratory illness in 26 countries between 2002 and 2003. It is believed that the basic reproductive number (R) of COVID19 – i.e. the number of new cases generated by each infected person – is between 2.0 and 3.0, higher than flu (1.3). As with the estimates of mortality rate, data is highly variable depending on the testing regime and social policies in force in each region or country. The test for the novel coronavirus is done in specialised laboratories. Specimens can be collected from the upper (nose and throat swabs) or lower (saliva and mucus samples) respiratory tracts. These specimens are sent to the reference laboratories for testing. The RNA in the samples is amplified and sequences which match with the genome of the novel coronavirus identified. That China released the sequence of the novel coronavirus genome early in the outbreak was greatly appreciated by scientists around the world.

Further Reading

Barton J (2019) *A History of the Bible: The book and its faiths*, Allen Lane, London

Bruce D and Bruce A (1998) *Engineering Genesis: The ethics of genetic engineering in non-human species*, Earthscan Publications Ltd, London

Carey N (2012) *The Epigenetics Revolution: How modern Biology is rewriting our understanding of genetics disease and inheritance*, Icon Books, London

Carey N (2020) *Hacking the Code of Life: How Gene Editing Will Rewrite our Futures*, Icon Books, London

Doudna J and Sternberg S (2017) *A Crack in Creation: New power to control evolution*, Bodley Head, London

Ellis J (2010) *How Science Works: Evolution*, Springer, Dordrecht

Francis RC (2011) *Epigenetics*, Norton, New York

Gawande A (2014) *Being Mortal: Illness, medicine, and what matters in the end*, Profile Books, London

Jones DA (2004) *The Soul of the Embryo: An inquiry into the status of the embryo in Christian tradition*, Continuum, London

Kumar S (2009) *Earth Pilgrim*, Green Books, Totness

Mann R (2012) *Dazzling Darkness: Gender, sexuality, illness and God*, Wild Goose Publications, Glasgow

McGrath A (2017) *The Great Mystery: Science, God and the human quest for meaning*, Hodder and Stoughton, London

McLeish T (2014) *Faith and Wisdom in Science*, OUP.

Parratt J (2020) *So We Live, Forever Bidding Farewell: Theology and Assisted Dying*, Sacristy Press, Durham

Pearson H (2016) *The Life Project: The extraordinary story of our ordinary lives*, Allen Lane, London

Skloot R (2010) *The Immortal life of Henrietta Lacks*, Macmillan, London

Spong JS (2018) *Unbelievable*, Harper, New York

Wyatt J (2009) *Matters of Life and Death: Human dilemmas in the light of Christian Faith*, Intervarsity Press, London

The Author: David Atkinson

A degree in Biology from the University of Hull, a PhD in Plant Ecology at the University of Newcastle upon Tyne was followed by employment as a research scientist at East Malling Research Station (now East Malling Research), Kent, the Macaulay Institute for Soil Research, Aberdeen (later the Macaulay Land Use Research Institute and now the James Hutton Institute), the University of Aberdeen and the Scottish Agricultural College, Edinburgh. Retirement from academic life was followed by study at the Theological Institute of the Scottish Episcopal Church and Ordination in 2005.

Over the period 1976 to 2008 there was significant involvement with the British Crop Protection Council (Now British Crop Production Council} and its international Conferences. This led to interest in issues linked to food quality such as the differences between organic and conventional and GM foods, and to a role in the development of the Scottish Government's 2010 Food Strategy. Studies of issues linked to GM foods led to a role, through the Church of Scotland's 'Science Religion and Technology Project', into work on Stem Cells and Nuclear Power. It also led to membership of the Royal College of Physicians of Edinburgh's Advisory Committee and to a period on the supervising Board for the Membership of the Royal College of Physicians qualification as a Lay Advisor.

Through the Scottish Episcopal Churches 'Church in Society Committee' there was work on Genome Editing which culminated in its discussion at the 2019 General Synod. Work in this area also involved attendance at a meeting of the Council of European Churches on 'Genome Editing' held in Paris in February 2018, which led to the establishment of an Anglican Bio-ethics Group to consider this and linked issues like Assisted Suicide.

The Templeton Foundation Programme on 'Scientists in Congregations' led to work on whether Pilgrimage could be a means of promoting discussion of Science-linked issues within families and church groups.

David is currently a non-stipendiary Priest working alongside the Revd Canon John Walker based in the Donside Group of Churches in Aberdeenshire.